THE
Holy Spirit
AND THE
Believer

by Theodore H. Epp
Director
Back to the Bible Broadcast

A
BACK TO THE BIBLE
PUBLICATION

Back to the Bible

Lincoln, Nebraska 68501

70,000 printed to date—1979
(5-8408—70M—39)
ISBN 0-8474-0718-7

Printed in the United States of America

Foreword

For 40 years the Back to the Bible Broadcast has systematically taught the Word of God from a conservative, evangelical viewpoint. Speakers on the program have not ignored theological areas in which Bible scholars differ but have spoken clearly and with conviction on controversial matters.

In recent years the role of the Holy Spirit in the life of the believer has been the subject of increasing study by Bible students of various persuasions. In this book we have brought together some of the most pertinent lessons on the Holy Spirit given by Back to the Bible's founder and director, Theodore H. Epp. This material is compiled from *The Other Comforter* (chs. 1-6), *Gifts of the Spirit* (chs. 7-9,11), *The Use and Abuse of Tongues* (ch. 10) and *Spiritual Gifts for Every Believer* (chs. 12,13). Each of these publications is available from Back to the Bible (see back cover).

—The Publishers

Contents

Introduction

The Holy Spirit is a member of the Trinity. He is a member of the Godhead, which consists of the Father, the Son and the Holy Spirit. It is essential that we as Christians learn to know the Holy Spirit, not as an influence as some would describe Him, but as a divine Person. This concept of Him will prepare us for the blessings that He wants to bring into our lives.

We might ask ourselves some questions concerning the Holy Spirit. Is He worthy of our adoration or of our faith or of our love? Is He to receive us and use us? Or are we to receive Him in order to use Him? Should we seek more of the Holy Spirit? Or should He have more of us? If we, at will, may have more of the Holy Spirit, we are likely to become proud. If, on the other hand, the Holy Spirit is the One who should have more of us, the likelihood is that we will become humble. For us to know Him as a divine Person to whom we should be in constant submission will lead to the transformation of our lives.

Chapter 1

Before and After Pentecost

The Holy Spirit is a divine Person, equal with the Father and with the Son in the Godhead. They are all equal in power and wisdom and majesty.

Where Does God Dwell?

There are great mysteries in connection with the Trinity that the human mind cannot explore. They are beyond the realm of our comprehension. Take for example the location of each member of the Trinity in the universe. The Bible speaks of the Father as being in heaven. That is His special residence. The Lord Jesus is at the right hand of the Father making intercession for His people. The Word of God tells us that the Holy Spirit is here on earth dwelling in the Church, the Body of Christ, and in believers. Yet, these three are so closely knit together that what thought comes to the mind of one is also on the minds of the others. They are inseparable and work together in perfect harmony and unity.

There was a time when the residence of the Lord Jesus Christ was not at the right hand of the Father but was here on earth. We learn in Galatians 4:4 that when the fullness of time was come, God sent forth His Son, made of a woman, made under

9

the Law. There was a definite time appointed for the incarnation of our Lord. Men waited for thousands of years for the promise of the Seed of the woman to be fulfilled, and one day it was. The appointed time arrived.

The Holy Spirit has not always had His special residence in the Church and in the child of God. His coming to take up His work was promised by our Lord (John 14:16,17). He instructed His disciples to wait in Jerusalem until the coming of the Spirit (Acts 1:4), and that coming took place at Pentecost (ch. 2). He had been in the world before, for He, as the other members of the Godhead, is omnipresent (present everywhere at the same time). But He took up a new work and a new residence at Pentecost.

The teaching in the Bible concerning the Holy Spirit is revealed in a progressive manner. The work and purposes of God are not disclosed to man all at one time. Truth is added to truth as the need arises.

Changing Methods

Moreover, God's methods of work may change and do change from time to time. He is unchanging in His Person, but He is not bound to do the same thing in one age that He did in another. For example, we learn from the Old Testament that the Spirit of God came upon whichever person He chose, regardless of the spiritual condition of that person. He acted as a free, sovereign agent, coming upon men as He willed. In some places we are told that He "entered" into a certain individual in order to do some special work. In other places we read how someone was "anointed by" the Spirit of God to do a particular work. We might speak of His work during that period as "selective indwelling." This could be used to describe both the persons He indwelt and the length of time He indwelt them.

It would seem that such individuals as Joseph, Daniel, Joshua and David were indwelt by the Holy Spirit without interruption. Yet David was aware that the Spirit of God could and would withdraw Himself from an individual under certain circumstances. In his prayer in Psalm 51, David cried out to God after seeing the terrible nature of his sins: "Take not thy holy spirit from me" (v. 11). This is not the kind of prayer we would pray today. This will be plain when we study the present work of the Holy Spirit as revealed in the New Testament.

David had the example of Saul before him when he pleaded with God not to take His Holy Spirit from him. When Saul set his will against the will of God, he was not only rejected as king, but "the Spirit of the Lord departed from . . . him" (I Sam. 16:14).

In the case of Samson it appears that the Spirit of God came upon him only on certain occasions. When some special work had to be done, then Samson was empowered to do it. However, when the mark of the Nazarite was removed from him by the cutting of his hair, we learn that "he wist not that the Lord was departed from him" (Judg. 16:20). It was only in answer to prayer on the part of Samson that the Lord gave him special power to destroy the house filled with the leaders of the Philistines (vv. 3-31).

11

Christ's Teaching About the Holy Spirit

During His earthly ministry the Lord Jesus Christ taught His disciples that they might receive the Holy Spirit through prayer to the Father. The record in Luke 11:13 is "If ye then, being evil, know how to give good gifts unto your children: how much more shall your heavenly Father give the Holy Spirit to them that ask him?" This was a new and staggering truth for a Jew to consider. It is evident from the Gospel records that Mary of Bethany was perhaps the only one who did ask for the Holy Spirit in accordance with this promise. Apparently none of the disciples did. Undoubtedly, they knew of a promise in Joel that a time would come when the Spirit of God would come upon men and women, but apparently they did not heed this promise of the Lord which would have given the Spirit in advance of the time referred to in Joel. This may explain why Mary alone, of all of Christ's followers, seemed to grasp what Christ meant by His repeated statements concerning His death and resurrection.

For us in this day and age to consider the promise of Luke 13 as being a promise for us now is to ignore the great truths concerning the Holy Spirit that relate to Pentecost and His indwelling of believers. The Bible teaches that every believer in this age has the Spirit of God indwelling him.

Toward the close of His earthly ministry the Lord Jesus promised that He would pray to the Father, and in answer to that prayer the Comforter, the Holy Spirit, would come and abide with believers: "And I will pray the Father, and he shall give you another Comforter, that he may abide with you for ever" (John 14:16). Here all three Persons of the Trinity are brought before us. There is the Lord Jesus, who prayed; the Father, to whom He prayed; and the Holy Spirit, who was to be sent by the Father in answer to our Lord's prayer. There is more than that, however, in this passage. Something new would be done by the Holy Spirit in answer to this prayer. He would not only come and indwell believers, but He would abide with them forever.

The next verse in this chapter says, "Even the Spirit of truth; whom the world cannot receive, because it seeth him not, neither knoweth him: but ye know him; for he dwelleth with you, and shall be in you." Two little prepositions here tell, in a progressive way, the story of the revelation concerning the Holy Spirit. Our Saviour said to His disciples that the Holy Spirit was with them, but an event would take place in the near future in which the Holy Spirit would indwell them and would abide with them forever. God's people even then were not without the help of the Holy Spirit, but His permanent indwelling of all believers was future to the conversation that our Lord had with His disciples in which this promise was made.

It was very possible on the first evening of His resurrection that our Lord found the disciples in the upper room. He breathed on them, saying, "Receive ye the Holy Ghost" (20:22). This may seem like a contradiction to some other Scriptures. For example, in Luke 24:49 we read: "And, behold, I send the promise of my Father upon you: but tarry ye in the city of Jerusalem, until ye be endued with power from on high."

The Spirit's Coming at Pentecost

That the disciples should wait for the fulfillment of the promise concerning the Holy Spirit is stated again in Acts 1:4,5. The Lord, "being assembled together with them, commanded them that they should not depart from Jerusalem, but wait for the promise of the Father, which, saith he, ye have heard of me. . . . Ye shall be baptized with the Holy Ghost not many days hence." Then, according to verse 8, they were to be endued with the power after the Holy Spirit came upon them, and they would be witnesses to Christ throughout the world.

There is no contradiction, however, between the Lord's breathing on them the Holy Spirit and these instructions to wait for the coming of the Holy Spirit. This breathing on them was an earnest of what was to happen in the very near future. Moreover, what happened to the few was going to take place in the lives of all who believed in Christ. It was not just the 12 but the whole body of believers on whom the Spirit came. This is what we find in Acts 2:1-4: "And when the day of Pentecost was fully come, they were all with one accord in one place. And suddenly there came a sound from heaven as of a rushing mighty wind, and it filled all the house where they were sitting. And there appeared unto them cloven tongues like as of fire, and it sat upon each of them. And they were all filled with the Holy Ghost, and began to speak with other tongues, as the Spirit gave them utterance."

This was a definite manifestation of the appearance of the third Person of the Trinity. Some 33

14

years preceding this Jesus Christ came to earth in the form of a baby in Bethlehem. These are both never-to-be-repeated steps. Christ will not come again as a child to Bethlehem, and Pentecost will not be repeated, for both were events predicted to take place at a certain time and at a certain place, and this was fulfilled.

The method of how the Spirit came upon believers was not always the same, according to the Book of the Acts. In a number of cases the Spirit came when believers laid their hands on those who had received Christ. This was true of Paul when Ananias visited him in Damascus. We are told, "Ananias went his way, and entered into the house; and putting his hands on him said, Brother Saul, the Lord, even Jesus, that appeared unto thee in the way as thou camest, hath sent me, that thou mightest receive thy sight, and be filled with the Holy Ghost" (9:17).

The same was true concerning certain disciples Paul found in Ephesus, persons who knew only of John's baptism and not of the coming of the Holy Spirit. Then, "When Paul had laid his hands upon them, the Holy Ghost came on them" (19:6). Paul and these disciples were converted Jews to whom the impartation of the Holy Spirit through the laying on of hands was apparently a special sign.

Another instance of this is recorded in Acts 8. Philip ministered in Samaria, and a revival broke out. Peter and John were sent from Jerusalem to find out what was going on, and when they came, they found the Samaritan believers and prayed for them "that they might receive the Holy Ghost: (For as yet he was fallen upon none of them: only they were baptized in the name of the Lord

15

Jesus)" (8:15,16). It was not until the apostles laid their hands on these Samaritan Christians that "they received the Holy Ghost" (v. 17).

These Samaritans were only part Jews, and a very good reason can be suggested for this delay in their receiving the Holy Spirit. The Samaritan woman with whom our Saviour spoke claimed for the Samaritans certain rights and privileges with regard to the worship of God which our Saviour denied. He said to her: "Ye worship ye know not what: we know what we worship: for salvation is of the Jews" (John 4:22).

It was a Jew that brought the message of salvation to the Samaritans, and it was two Jews, Peter and John, whom God used to impart to these Samaritan believers the Holy Spirit. It was not that converted Jews could save the Samaritans but that God had given Israel a special place in His program, and He emphasized this through a Jewish evangelist's bringing the Word and through the fact that two Jewish Christian leaders imparted the Holy Spirit to these new converts.

Moreover, it was not God's intention that there would be a Jewish Church and a Samaritan Church; they were to be one body in Christ.

The events in the household of Cornelius differed from these three instances where the Holy Spirit was given by the laying on of hands. In the case of Cornelius and his household, it was while Peter spoke the words of life that "the Holy Ghost fell on all them which heard the word" (Acts 10:44).

Peter was apparently wise with the wisdom of the Spirit in taking six Jewish brethren along with him when he went to the home of this Gentile. We

16

learn: "And they of the circumcision which believed were astonished, as many as came with Peter, because that on the Gentiles also was poured out the gift of the Holy Ghost" (v. 45). This had its effect upon the church in Jerusalem when some of the Christian Jews contended with Peter because he had gone into a Gentile's house and had eaten with him. Peter had witnesses to prove that when he began to speak, the Holy Spirit, as he said, "fell on them, as on us at the beginning. Then remembered I the word of the Lord, how that he said, John indeed baptized with water; but ye shall be baptized with the Holy Ghost. Forasmuch then as God gave them the like gift as he did unto us, who believed on the Lord Jesus Christ; what was I, that I could withstand God?" (11:15-17). Peter did not lay his hands on these Gentiles in order to impart the Holy Spirit, but God imparted the Holy Spirit to them as Peter preached the Word. What was done was done directly by God. This was proof to the Jewish Christians that God had received these Gentiles into His family.

When the Spirit Comes to Individuals

In this we see different methods God used to impart the Holy Spirit to believers. In the case of those on whom hands were laid before they received the Holy Spirit, they became believers and then were given the Spirit of God. In the case of Cornelius' household, the Spirit was given apparently at the time the people believed. Some teach that the Spirit always takes up His residence in the believer at a time subsequent to salvation. This is not the case. The Book of the Acts itself contains the answer, and it is corroborated in some of the epistles.

In the King James Version Acts 19:2 begins, "He said unto them, Have ye received the Holy Ghost since ye believed?" The New American Standard Bible translates this portion correctly in the following words: "Did you receive the Holy Spirit when you believed?" The New Berkeley Version is similar in rendering the section this way: "Did you receive the Holy Spirit on your becoming believers?" From this language we conclude that Paul expected believers at that time to receive the Holy Spirit upon their acceptance of Christ and not at some future time. A number of years had elapsed since Pentecost, and the work of God was being fit into the pattern it would follow down through the years of this dispensation.

A similar passage is Ephesians 1:13. It reads in the King James Version: "In whom ye also trusted, after that ye heard the word of truth, the gospel of your salvation: in whom also after that ye believed, ye were sealed with that Holy Spirit of promise." Here, as in Acts 19:2, this portion should be translated: "In whom also upon believing ye were sealed with the Holy Spirit of promise," or, "When ye believed ye were sealed with the Holy Spirit of promise."

In subsequent chapters the different works of the Holy Spirit will be pointed out, but it is essential now to see that the impartation of the Holy Spirit in this day and age is at the moment of the individual's acceptance of Christ as personal Saviour.

Chapter 2

Why Was the Holy Spirit Sent?

Two verses in John's Gospel provide the answers as to who sent the Holy Spirit and why: "And I will pray the Father, and he shall give you another Comforter, that he may abide with you for ever" (14:16). "But the Comforter, which is the Holy Ghost, whom the Father will send in my name, he shall teach you all things" (v. 26). From these we learn that God the Father and the Lord Jesus Christ united in sending the Holy Spirit. Usually in a case where one person is sent by another to do a certain task, the one sending is superior to the one sent. We say, "usually," because there are exceptions, and this is one of those exceptions. In the work of redemption the Son and the Holy Spirit at times subordinate themselves to the Father, though in the Godhead all three are equal.

According to these Scriptures, however, the Holy Spirit subordinates Himself to the will of the Father and to the will of the Son in working out the benefits of redemption for us. What had proved to be impossible under the Law, because we could not obey the Law, is possible under the gospel. The Lord Jesus was going to enter into the presence of the Father to perform a special task on our behalf, and the Holy Spirit was sent to the earth to work in our hearts to perform another aspect of that work.

19

To Impart Christ's Life

Ever since the fall of man God has demonstrated in many different ways that man does not have the power in himself to do what he ought to do to please God. Man was created innocent, yet at the first temptation he fell. Man was not able to stand unaided and live a spiritual life in keeping with God's standards. With the coming of Jesus Christ to save man the whole picture changed. The Eternal God became man in the Person of Jesus Christ in order to provide salvation for us.

While here on the earth He proved that a sinless life was possible. Now He continues to live to demonstrate that His life in us will not fail to fulfill its God-ordained purpose. This new life is Christ Himself, whose life is brought out in us through the Holy Spirit.

It was necessary in the working out of this new life in us that we be made free from that which entangles us in sin. Provision was made for this according to Romans 8:2: "For the law of the Spirit of life in Christ Jesus hath made me free from the law of sin and death." Just as a person can be made free from the law of gravity by calling into operation other laws, so we are made free from the principle, or the law, of sin and death, which, until the time of our trusting in Christ, held us down in sin.

The Law of Moses could never bring us this release. It was weak because we are weak. However, God sent His Son in the likeness, or guise, of sinful flesh and condemned sin (v. 3). God broke sin's power so that we may no longer be enslaved by it. But God not only made this provision through Christ, He also sent the Holy Spirit into our lives to make this work of Christ effective in our daily Christian experience.

Still more is needed, however. Christ went to the throne of the Father in order to do a work for us also. Why He is there becomes clear as we read I John 2:1: "My little children, these things write I unto you, that ye sin not. And if any man sin, we have an advocate with the Father, Jesus Christ the righteous." Thus we not only need a divine Person within us to make actual the new life in Christ, but we also need a divine Person before the throne of God to plead for us when we sin. In this way the work of Christ for our salvation is preserved since it does not rest on us but on Him.

Consider again the work of the Holy Spirit. He came to be a Comforter in the sense that our Lord Himself was a Comforter. When He spoke of the Holy Spirit as "another Comforter," our Lord was saying that the Holy Spirit was a Comforter of the same nature and kind as He Himself is. The word "Comforter" means someone called alongside to help. This means more than someone taking us by the hand and giving us aid. It includes providing us with divine energy and divine life so that we become more like Christ.

For Fruitbearing

We have been chosen of God to represent Christ on this earth. This is not a choice we made but one our Saviour made. He said in John 15:16: "Ye have not chosen me, but I have chosen you, and ordained you, that ye should go and bring forth fruit, and that your fruit should remain: that whatsoever ye shall ask of the Father in my name, he may give it you." We have been chosen for the purpose of bringing forth fruit, something impossible for us to fulfill on our own. We need the help of the Holy Spirit to carry this out.

The Apostle Paul deals with this subject in Romans 12, where he says, "For as we have many members in one body, and all members have not the same office: so we, being many, are one body in Christ, and every one members one of another" (Rom. 12:4,5).

The same truth is set forth in I Corinthians 12:14-21. Here we are reminded that the body is not one member but many members. "If the foot shall say, Because I am not the hand, I am not of the body" (v. 15). The apostle speaks of the ear and the eye in the same manner and then concludes, "But now hath God set the members every one of them in the body, as it hath pleased him" (v. 18). We are all placed in the Body of Christ to do a special task, and we need each other for that. The Spirit of God divides to each member of the Body individually, according to His will. We are each given a certain aspect of the work that must be done; and if each person does his task, we function as do the members of the human body. We cannot get along without each other. I need you and you need me.

Not everyone is called to do all the preaching or all the teaching or all the leading. There are certain things all of us can do that are the same, but there are some things that each of us do differently. It is in the province of the Holy Spirit to see that each of us is able to accomplish the work laid upon us so that there will be no failure in the work of God.

The Lord Jesus Christ is concerned with seeing that the work is done for us and shall be successful in us. He leaves no room for failure. We have been called by Him and chosen to go and bring forth fruit that will last. It will be permanent. This is possible only because the Holy Spirit has been sent to dwell in us and to work out in us the will and purposes of God. Since He dwells in us for that purpose, we have the responsibility of letting Him control us so that His work in us will go on unhindered.

It was this that our Saviour had reference to when He said in John 7:37,38: "If any man thirst, let him come after me, and drink. He that believeth on me, as the scripture hath said, out of his belly [innermost being] shall flow rivers of living water." The Spirit of God dwells in us to bring this to realization in our lives.

When the Lord Jesus was discussing with His disciples the subject of sending them the Holy Spirit, He said in John 14:18: "I will not leave you comfortless: I will come to you." From this word "comfortless" we get our word "orphan." The word in the Greek means someone who is left desolate or bereft of any help or assistance. In the plan of God for society, parents help their children, and in the family of God, the Holy Spirit is here to help the believer in this very way.

Our Lord said at one time, "I live," and He added "Ye shall live also" (John 14:19). This accords with Romans 5:10, where we learn that we are reconciled by the death of Jesus Christ and that we shall live by His life. This is His resurrection

23

life, which only the Holy Spirit can produce in us. This is why Paul could say in II Corinthians 4:10,11 that he always bore about in his body the dying of the Lord Jesus, that the life also of Jesus "might be made manifest in [his] body." The Spirit of God has come to identify us with a divine life here so that we can be identified with our Lord before the Father.

Peter tells us that God has given us "all things that pertain unto life and godliness, through the knowledge of him that hath called us to glory and virtue" (II Pet. 1:3). The verse that follows says, "Whereby are given unto us exceeding great and precious promises: that by these ye might be partakers of the divine nature" (v. 4). From God's standpoint there is nothing to hinder the expression in us of the new life in Christ.

It is the work of the Holy Spirit to identify us with the life of the Lord Jesus Christ. The Spirit came to teach us, to give peace, to give courage, to give testimony, to guide us into all truth and to pray through us. He is God's free gift of grace to us at this time. He will not be withdrawn from us because He is to dwell with us forever.

The Lord Jesus Christ had to return to the Father before the Holy Spirit could come. In speaking to the disciples our Lord said, "Nevertheless I tell you the truth; It is expedient for you that I go away: for if I go not away, the Comforter will not come unto you; but if I depart, I will send him unto you" (John 16:7). In looking into the future prophetic program of God, we see that the Holy Spirit must return to heaven with the Church to present us to the Lord Jesus Christ and the Father before the Saviour returns the second time to the earth.

Three Works of the Spirit

In my early years in the ministry, I was very perplexed concerning the teaching of the Bible on the Holy Spirit until I read a book entitled, *The Threefold Secret of the Holy Spirit*, by James McConkey. He summarized the work of the Holy Spirit in the heart of the believer under three headings: (1) The Secret of His Incoming; (2) The Secret of His Fullness; (3) The Secret of His Constant Manifestation.

The secret of the incoming of the Holy Spirit has to do with His regenerating work and His baptizing the believer into the Body of Christ. We have already covered this, but the following summary will help us crystallize these truths in a way that we will not forget them. The new birth is the work of the Holy Spirit within us. Through His regenerating power He imparts to us the divine nature. We have already learned from Romans 8 that when a person is born again, the Holy Spirit enters his heart and forms Christ in him. Christ becomes the believer's life. The person who does not have the Spirit of God is not a child of God. This, in brief, covers the subject of the secret of His incoming.

Some Christians struggle with God, asking that they might receive the Holy Spirit, not realizing that He indwelt them from the moment they were born again. It is wrong for us to plead with God for the incoming of the Holy Spirit after we have accepted Christ as personal Saviour, for we are asking God to do what He has already done.

The second aspect of His work within us has to do with His infilling, or His fullness. It is one thing for Him to make His home in our hearts, it is another thing for Him to control our lives. It is one thing to receive the Holy Spirit. It is another thing to be filled with the Holy Spirit. When we surrender ourselves to Him, He takes possession of us.

This infilling of the Holy Spirit does not go unchallenged because when He seeks to take over the center of our lives, there is opposition from the flesh nature within us. This is what Paul tells us in Galatians when he says, "The flesh lusteth [desires] against the Spirit, and the Spirit against the flesh" (Gal. 5:17). These two are contrary to one another so that we cannot do the things we would like to do. This conflict begins the moment the Holy Spirit comes into our hearts. It is His desire that we might be completely controlled by Him so that our behavior honors God.

It is our duty and privilege to surrender our bodies to Him. This is the message of Romans 6:13: "Neither yield ye your members as instruments of unrighteousness unto sin: but yield yourselves unto God, as those that are alive from the dead, and your members as instruments of righteousness unto God." The same truth is found in Romans 12:1, where we are told to present our bodies a living sacrifice unto God. Unless we do this, the Holy Spirit will not be able to fill our lives completely.

The surrender of some of us might be compared to a person entering a ten-room house and being allowed into only two or three of the rooms but not into any of the others. This is often how we fail the Holy Spirit in surrendering our lives to

Him. Let us yield to Him in every area of our lives that He brings to our minds. We make a sad mistake when we wait for the Holy Spirit to take possession. He is waiting for us to act in obedience to God to permit His complete possession.

The third aspect is the secret of the outflowing, or constant manifestation, of the Holy Spirit. A well-known passage which teaches this truth is John 7:37-39: "In the last day, that great day of the feast, Jesus stood and cried, saying, If any man thirst, let him come unto me, and drink. He that believeth on me, as the scripture hath said, out of his belly shall flow rivers of living water. (But this spake he of the Spirit, which they that believe on him should receive: for the Holy Ghost was not yet given; because that Jesus was not yet glorified.)" This is the normal outcome in a life that has been regenerated, that has been possessed by the Spirit and then is empowered for service.

In His conversation with the woman at the well, our Lord said, "But whosoever drinketh of the water that I shall give him shall never thirst; but the water that I shall give him shall be in him a well of water springing up into everlasting life" (4:14). The figure our Saviour used shows us that the coming of the Spirit is not the end of His work but that He will fill us to the place where, like a spring of water, we will overflow with refreshment for others.

It means more than this, however. This has reference not only to witnessing and ministry but also to the fruit of the Spirit becoming a reality in our experiences and overflowing to the benefit of others. That fruit is "love, joy, peace, longsuffering,

27

gentleness, goodness, faith, meekness, temperance: against such there is no law" (Gal. 5:22,23).

The fruit of the Spirit was seen in such men as John and Paul. They both reflected Christ in their lives in similar ways and also in divergent ways.

It was true also of their ministries. They were both gifted of God for special service but in different ways. This is in keeping with what we are told in I Corinthians 12. The Spirit of God gives "to every man severally as he will" (v. 11). At the direction of the Spirit, each of us is gifted to minister in one way or another the gospel to others. This all has to do with the outflowing of the Spirit in our lives. There are different kinds of ministries but the same Spirit.

The results of the filling of the Holy Spirit are many. One of these is that we receive power to do God's work. Another is that we receive knowledge, for He reveals to us the things that Christ has spoken for our good. Then there is fruitfulness in that the fruit of the Spirit is manifested in us and God gives the increase to our witness for Him.

This places the obligation on us to surrender ourselves fully to the Lord. Only as we do this can He fill us or control us to where our lives overflow with His life, making the water of life available to others.

Chapter 3

Sealed and Indwelt by the Spirit

One of the key verses relating to this sealing of the Holy Spirit is Ephesians 1:13: "In whom ye also trusted, after that ye heard the word of truth, the gospel of your salvation: in whom also after that ye believed, ye were sealed with that holy Spirit of promise." This truth is also stated in II Corinthians 1:22: "Who hath also sealed us, and given the earnest of the Spirit in our hearts."

God the Father is the agent who seals the Son according to John 6:27. And He is the one who has anointed us and has sealed us according to II Corinthians 1:21.

The ones sealed are those who have trusted in Christ. This is clear from the Scriptures already quoted. The basis for this is believing the gospel of Christ. When that is believed, Christ is received, the Holy Spirit comes into the believer, and God seals the believer by the Spirit. The Holy Spirit is given to us as the earnest of our further inheritance.

The Word of God does not say that the Spirit is given only to the spiritual Christian. It is possible for believers to become carnal; nevertheless, they are sealed by the Spirit of God. Paul told the Corinthians that he could not write to them as unto spiritual "but as unto carnal, even as unto babes in Christ" (I Cor. 3:1). Yet it was to this same group that he wrote in his second letter: "Now he which

29

stablisheth us with you in Christ, and hath anointed us, is God; who hath also sealed us, and given the earnest of the Spirit in our hearts" (II Cor. 1:21,22).

Sealing has nothing to do with behavior. The sealing takes place at the time of the new birth, and we never become unsealed. Never in the Bible are we exhorted to be sealed. We are admonished to be filled with the Spirit, but not once are we commanded to be sealed. The sealing automatically follows our being born from above. It is universal to all believers, but with it goes an exhortation not to grieve the Holy Spirit now that we are sealed by Him. This is the message of Ephesians 4:30: "And grieve not the holy Spirit of God, whereby ye are sealed unto the day of redemption."

We have stated that the believer is sealed the moment that he believes, but some might point to Ephesians 1:13 as teaching something other than this. Instead of "In whom also *after* that ye believed, ye were sealed with that holy Spirit of promise" (KJV), it should read: "In whom *upon* believing, or *having* believed, ye were sealed with that Holy Spirit of promise." This tells us that the sealing was an instantaneous act at the time of regeneration. At the moment we were born again the Holy Spirit entered and became the seal of God on our lives.

Purpose of Sealing

What is the purpose of God's sealing us with the Holy Spirit? First of all, sealing signifies a finished transaction. God is saying, in effect, that the matter of our salvation is finished or as good as completed. In Philippians 1:6 we learn: "He which hath begun a good work in you will perform it [finish it]." Consequently, the sealing speaks of a finished transaction.

In the second place, it speaks of ownership. Sealing is the mark of God upon the believer. The rancher who puts a brand on his cattle does so to signify his ownership. When Christ asked his disciples whose insignia was on a coin and was given the answer, "Caesar's," He said that they were to give to Caesar that which was Caesar's and to God that which was God's (see Matt. 22:19-21). Since it is a mark of ownership, the sealing of the Holy Spirit becomes the earnest of our inheritance. It is God's pledge and a foretaste of the good things He has for us in the future.

Sealing also speaks of authority. In the Old Testament we read that Pharaoh gave Joseph a ring and the King of Persia gave a ring to Mordecai. Just so, God has given us His Spirit to mark us with authority. According to Ephesians 2:5,6 we have been raised together with Christ into a place of responsibility and authority.

Finally, the sealing of the Holy Spirit signifies security. This should encourage those who, though they have trusted Christ, are still fearful in regard to these matters.

The sealing of the believer for security is a very precious aspect of this great truth. Like any doctrine of the Word, the teaching on the believer's security can be misrepresented. Let us be careful not to deny ourselves the blessings of this truth, however, just because some have abused it.

We read in Daniel 6 that the king sealed the stones which marked the exit to the lion's den in

31

which Daniel was placed. Only the king himself dared break those seals. The Romans sealed the sepulcher in which the body of Jesus was placed so that none would dare open it. These, however, were seals placed by men, and God is not bound by such insufficient seals.

With regard to the Holy Spirit's being our seal, Ephesians 1:14 says, "Which is the earnest of our inheritance until the redemption of the purchased possession, unto the praise of his glory." The word "until" assures us that the Spirit of God is the seal of our inheritance until the redemption of the body. This is the day of redemption spoken of in Ephesians 4:30, where we are told: "And grieve not the holy Spirit of God, whereby ye are sealed unto the day of redemption."

There are three different phases of redemption, the first being redemption from the guilt of sin. This took place when we were born again, or regenerated. We are redeemed from the power of sin in this life when we allow the Holy Spirit to control us. We will be redeemed from the very presence of sin at the coming of the Lord Jesus when He takes us away to be with Himself. The Spirit of God is the guarantee that we will be kept to that glorious day.

The confirmation of this is given in I Peter 1:5: "Who [the children of God] are kept by the power of God through faith unto salvation ready to be revealed in the last time." This is God's guarantee to the believer of eternal life, but this does not mean that we can do as we (i.e., the old nature) please and not suffer the consequences. We are warned not to grieve the Spirit of God, and many

Scripture passages tell us that God severely chastens His children when necessary.

Only God can break the seal that He Himself has established. Any seal that a man makes God can break, but any seal God makes only He can break. God has promised He will not break this seal, for the seal is the Holy Spirit, and His presence with us is the assurance of our security unto the day of redemption. This sealing, as we have pointed out before, is only for those who have turned in faith to Christ and have been regenerated. Let us not build false hopes on human merit or on any system of salvation other than salvation by grace through faith in Christ (Eph. 2:8,9).

The Indwelling of the Holy Spirit

There is possibly no clearer truth in the New Testament than that the believer is indwelt by the Holy Spirit. Paul wrote to the Corinthians: "Know ye not that ye are the temple of God, and that the Spirit of God dwelleth in you?" (I Cor. 3:16). In Chapter 6 and verse 19 of the same book he wrote, "Know ye not that your body is the temple of the Holy Ghost which is in you, which ye have of God, and ye are not your own?" Of the fact of the Holy Spirit's indwelling there can be no doubt.

Why does the Spirit of God indwell the believer? What is the purpose of His incoming? An answer is given in Romans 8:9-11: "But ye are not in the flesh, but in the Spirit, if so be that the Spirit of God dwell in you. Now if any man have not the Spirit of Christ, he is none of his. And if Christ be in you, the body is dead because of sin;

33

but the Spirit is life because of righteousness. But if the Spirit of him that raised up Jesus from the dead dwell in you, he that raised up Christ from the dead shall also quicken your mortal bodies by his Spirit that dwelleth in you." The purpose, then, of His indwelling is that He might cause us to live in righteousness. Before our salvation we were dead in trespasses and sins. The absence of the Spirit of God in any life is evidence enough of the unsaved condition of that life. For, "If any man have not the Spirit of Christ, he is none of his" (v. 9).

Jude, in his epistle, wrote about a certain unsaved class of people in these words: "These be they who separate themselves, sensual, having not the Spirit" (1:19). The word "sensual" is exactly the same word that is used in I Corinthians 2:14 and is translated "natural." It refers to the unsaved man. The natural man does not receive the things of the Spirit of God for the simple reason that the Spirit of God has not taken up His abode in such a life. Just as the absence of the Holy Spirit in a life speaks of the unsaved condition of that person, so the presence of the Holy Spirit is the evidence of life and the gift of God to the believer.

This means that if the Holy Spirit is in us, He produces the kind of life that God wants us to have. If the Holy Spirit is not in us, we are still in an unsaved condition. All believers are indwelt by the Holy Spirit. This does not necessarily mean that all believers are filled, or controlled by, the Holy Spirit. We must be careful to note the difference between the indwelling of the Spirit and the filling, or the controlling, by the Spirit.

The indwelling of the Holy Spirit does not depend on our consciousness of that indwelling.

Whether we feel we are indwelt or feel we are not indwelt has nothing to do with it. We are the temple of God, and the Spirit of God dwells in us according to I Corinthians 3:16. This is not qualified by whether or not we feel like it. This is a truth for every believer. Since God says this is so, it is so.

Even the carnal Christian is indwelt by the Spirit of God. Though carnal, he is still a believer. This was true of the Corinthians (v. 1); they needed to be awakened to the truth of the Holy Spirit's indwelling presence.

Indwelling Is Not Filling

The consequences of remaining carnal when God has made clear His truth to us should cause us to search our hearts. The Word says, "If any man defile the temple of God, him shall God destroy" (v. 17). This could mean physical death. Whether or not we consider them to be such, God says our bodies are holy since He has made them His temple. We are bought with a price; therefore, we should glorify God in our bodies and in our spirits, which are God's. We are warned in Ephesians 4:30, "Grieve not the holy Spirit of God, whereby ye are sealed unto the day of redemption." In the light of these things we dare not take this truth lightly.

We must realize, however, that our basis for the indwelling Spirit is faith in Christ as our Saviour, not our behavior. The filling of the Holy Spirit has to do with our behavior, but His indwelling has to do with our first act of faith when we trusted in Christ. His indwelling is a permanent matter. It is a once-for-all thing. This truth is also a factor in our assurance. The Lord Jesus said, "I will pray the Father, and he shall give you another Comforter, that he may abide with you for ever" (John 14:16). A little later He said to the disciples that the Spirit of God was with them; He said, "He . . . shall be in you" (v. 17).

Sin does not expel the Holy Spirit from our lives, but without fail it will bring conviction to our hearts. For the Holy Spirit to remove Himself when a Christian sins would be to leave that Christian without conviction and without life. If this were possible, it would mean he would be unborn, and the new birth would have to be repeated over and over again.

Every time we sin, it is the filling with the Holy Spirit and the power that is affected by sin, not the indwelling. The evidence for the indwelling Spirit is not our experience but the Word of God. He declares it, and that should settle it. He cannot lie. He would not deceive us. We are not to look for fruit as the evidence of the indwelling, but we are to believe God. The fruit of the Spirit, on the other hand, will be witnessed when we are controlled by the Holy Spirit.

Problem Passages

Consider now a few problem passages with regard to the subject of the Holy Spirit's indwelling, such as Acts 5:32: "And we are his witnesses of these things; and so is also the Holy Ghost, whom God hath given to them that obey him." Let us not jump to conclusions and think that the Spirit of God is given as the result of a life of obedience in the believer. The divine commentary on this is Acts

6:7: "And the word of God increased; and the number of the disciples multiplied in Jerusalem greatly; and a great company of the priests were obedient to the faith." This is the obedience Peter had reference to in Acts 5:32. There he spoke to unbelieving leaders of Israel and said that if they would obey the faith concerning Jesus Christ, they would be saved.

The same truth is brought out in Romans 1:5: "By whom we have received grace and apostleship, for obedience to the faith among all nations." It is clear, then, from these verses in Acts that the Spirit of God begins His indwelling work as a result of the believer's trusting Christ for salvation.

There are incidents in the Scriptures where there appears to be a temporary indwelling, but a careful study will indicate that every such case occurred before Pentecost. The Holy Spirit did not work before Pentecost in the way He did afterward in this regard. We see that in connection with Saul, from whom the Spirit of God departed. David had real cause to plead, after his grievous sins, that God would not take the Holy Spirit from him. These men did not have the promise we have today that the Spirit of God will dwell with the believer forever.

Chapter 4

The Baptism of the Holy Spirit

Three short passages of Scripture will form our background for our study on the subject of the baptism of the Holy Spirit. In his first letter to the Corinthians, Paul wrote, "For by one Spirit are we all baptized into one body" (12:13). We read in Romans 6:3: "Know ye not, that so many of us as were baptized into Jesus Christ were baptized into his death?" The third passage is Galatians 3:27: "For as many of you as have been baptized into Christ have put on Christ."

Baptism Defined

The word "baptize" is not an English word. We use it because we find it in our English translations of the Bible. It is a Greek word that has been transliterated; that is, it has been brought over bodily from the Greek into the English without being translated at all. There are various forms of the Greek word, such as *baptizo* and *bapto*. This word has two meanings which are very important to us who study the New Testament. The first meaning is "to submerge" in the sense that one would submerge a boat in water. It can also mean to be "overwhelmed in calamities." This is the way our Saviour used it when He said, "I have a baptism to be baptized with" (Luke 12:50). He was not talking about submerging something, such as a boat, in water but of being overwhelmed by calamities. In His case it was death on the cross.

The late Professor Kenneth S. Wuest, of the Moody Bible Institute of Chicago, a student and teacher of New Testament Greek, gives this further definition of the word translated "baptize": "The introduction or placing of a person or a thing into a new environment or into union with something else so as to alter its condition or its relationship to its previous environment or condition."

According to Matthew 3:11, John the Baptist said, "I indeed baptize you with water unto repentance: but he that cometh after me is mightier than I, whose shoes I am not worthy to bear: he shall baptize you with the Holy Ghost, and with fire." Baptism with fire has to do with the people of Israel in the Tribulation, when they will be submerged or overwhelmed by terrible calamities. But the baptism in the Spirit means something entirely different. It is a submergence, but of a different nature.

According to I Corinthians 12:13, we are baptized by one Spirit into one body. This means that the Holy Spirit places us or introduces us as believers into the Body of which Christ is the living Head. This is not His physical resurrection body, which is now glorified. In that body He is sitting at the right hand of the Father making intercession for us. The body spoken of in this passage in I Corinthians is the mystical Body of which every believer is a member. We became members of that Body by being placed into it by the Holy Spirit. This baptismal work by the Spirit took place at Pentecost when the Body of Christ was formed.

This becomes an actual fact in our lives the moment we are born again.

Again we must be careful to distinguish between things that are not the same. The baptism of the Spirit and the filling of the Spirit are different works of the Holy Spirit. If we do not note the differences involved, we will have nothing but confusion. In fact, a great deal of confusion with regard to the teaching on the Holy Spirit can be traced to this very thing.

Our Lord promised, according to Acts 1:5, "For John truly baptized with water; but ye shall be baptized with [or in] the Holy Ghost not many days hence." By using the words "not many days hence," our Lord was speaking of a particular time when this event would take place, namely Pentecost.

The Greek preposition translated "with" in Acts 1:5 can also be translated "in" or "by." Some persons have created confusion by insisting that only one of these is the correct meaning, whereas it could be any one of the three. We should be careful, however, to translate the preposition consistently in related passages.

This baptism with the Holy Spirit does not bring the Spirit to us, but rather puts the believer into a vital union with Christ through the work of the Holy Spirit. He came into this world from the Father at Pentecost to indwell the believer. But that was not all He did. He also took the believers and placed them, or submerged them, into the Body of Christ. In this way we become one with Christ, members of His mystical Body.

A brother in Christ used an illustration some years ago that I shall never forget. He reminded us that when copper and zinc, two different metals, are united, they form another metal known as brass. After brass has been produced, we cannot, by the same scientific process, separate the copper and the zinc, for they have become one. Through the baptism with the Spirit we become one with Christ as members of His Body of which He is the Head.

Being baptized by the Spirit into the Body of Christ does not automatically provide the power we need to live the Christian life or to serve the Lord. Through the baptism we are placed in the relationship with Christ that makes it possible for us to be empowered by Him.

Paul said to the Philippians, "I can do all things through Christ which strengtheneth me" (4:13). This power or strength is exercised by us because of the presence of the Spirit within us. But this is due to a work of the Holy Spirit other than His baptismal work. Our Lord said, "But ye shall receive power, after that the Holy Ghost is come upon you" (Acts 1:8). The enduement with power and the baptism of the Spirit are not identical, though one is dependent on the other. The placing of the believer into the Body of Christ was necessary before the power for living the Christian life was available. These then are two different phases of the Spirit's work.

Sometimes the work of the Holy Spirit and the work of Christ are so closely related in the Scriptures that it is hard for us to distinguish between them. Our Lord said concerning the Holy Spirit, "He shall glorify me: for he shall receive of mine, and shall shew it unto you. All things that the Father hath are mine: therefore said I, that he shall

41

take of mine, and shall shew it unto you" (John 16:14,15).

In John 7:37-39, our Lord said that if any man thirst, he should come to Him and drink. To the one who would believe he promised, "Out of his belly shall flow rivers of living water. (But this spake he of the Spirit, . . . [who] was not yet given.)" Thus by our placing faith in Christ, the work of the Spirit is made possible in our lives, and then through us He ministers to others.

As a spark ignites the gasoline-air mixture in the cylinders of an automobile motor to produce power, so the Holy Spirit produces the power of Christ's resurrection in us as human beings. First, however, we have to be united to Christ, and this is done as we are baptized into the one Body. Then it is possible for the Holy Spirit to do an additional work in making our life in Jesus Christ real to us and in us. Being baptized into the Body of Christ is a sure basis for holy, victorious and powerful living, because it puts us into the right relationship with Christ. Before these things can become a reality in our experience, we must respond in obedience to the Spirit's dealing in our lives. This is where the infilling is involved.

Baptismal Work Unique

According to Acts 1:5, the baptism with the Holy Spirit was only a few days away from the time the Lord Jesus, in His post-resurrection ministry, said, "Ye shall be baptized with the Holy Ghost not many days hence." At a later time, in vindicating His ministry to the Gentiles, Peter said to the early church leaders in Jerusalem: "As I began to speak, the Holy Ghost fell on them, as on us at the beginning. Then remembered I the word of the Lord, how that he said, John indeed baptized with water; but ye shall be baptized with the Holy Ghost. Forasmuch then as God gave them the like gift as he did unto us, who believed on the Lord Jesus Christ; what was I, that I could withstand God?" (11:15-17). In this Peter identified Pentecost as the fulfillment of the promise of the baptismal work of the Holy Spirit.

The Holy Spirit has been active in every dispensation, but His baptismal work is confined to this Church Age only. Only in this dispensation are believers in Christ made members of the Body of Christ.

Being baptized into the Body of Christ is not confined to certain believers in this age but is universal to all. Every genuine believer in Christ was baptized by the Holy Spirit into the Body of Christ the moment he believed. In writing to the Corinthians Paul was writing to both carnal and spiritual believers and said that all were baptized into the Body of Christ (I Cor. 12:13). Then in Ephesians 4:5 he pointed out that there is but one baptism that is on the same level and in the same category as one Lord and one faith, and that one baptism is for all believers.

As we have pointed out before, there is no command in the Bible for anyone to be baptized in the Holy Spirit. Believers are exhorted to be filled with the Holy Spirit but not to be baptized in the Holy Spirit. This is something that takes place the moment each person believes and is the basis for the filling of the Spirit. Potentially, the baptism of the Holy Spirit took place for all believers at Pente-

43

cost. Experientially—that is, as far as your experience and mine are concerned as believers—the baptism took place the moment we trusted Christ.

Another factor concerning the baptism of the Holy Spirit is that it is not a special experience of emotion because, like justification, it is a positional work, an objective work, not something that can be seen or felt by us.

Through the baptism of the Holy Spirit each of us becomes an individual member in the Body of Christ. This is what Paul said to the Corinthians: "Know ye not that your bodies are the members of Christ?" (6:15). This demands unity in the body. I have many members in my physical body with perfect unity among them. This is what God intends with regard to all who are individual members of the Body of Christ. All who are born again, whether they are from Africa or China or Russia or Japan or the Philippines or Europe or America, it makes no difference, they are all one in Christ.

Concerning this matter, Paul wrote: "But now hath God set the members every one of them in the body, as it hath pleased him" (I Cor. 12:18). Then, arguing for their diversity as well as their unity, the apostle says, "And if they were all one member, where were the body? But now are they many members, yet but one body" (vv. 19,20).

A basic purpose of the unity is seen beginning with verse 25: "That there should be no schism in the body; but that the members should have the same care one for another. And whether one member suffer, all the members suffer with it; or one member be honoured, all the members rejoice with it. Now ye are the body of Christ, and members in particular" (vv. 25-27). Judging from the way many believers live, this might seem to be a mistranslation. How many of us suffer with those of our fellow-Christians who suffer or rejoice with those who rejoice? If we do not, it is because we are not acting in the spirit of the Lord Jesus. It is because we do not allow the Holy Spirit to control our lives.

There should be perfect unity in the Body because there is only one head, Christ Himself. The Holy Spirit is the administrator to see that the life is available for every part of the Body. To say it another way, the Holy Spirit energizes every individual believer who makes up the Body of Christ.

The baptism of the Holy Spirit also has consequences with regard to the fallen nature within each one of us. In Romans 6:3 Paul said, "Know ye not, that so many of us as were baptized into Jesus Christ were baptized into his death?" Then in verse 6, we are told, "Knowing this, that our old man is crucified with him, that the body of sin might be destroyed [made inactive], that henceforth we should not serve sin."

There are those among God's people who say they want to die to self. Positionally before God these persons have already died to self, since the Bible tells us that all believers died together with Jesus Christ. The Holy Spirit is given to us, however, to make effective that work in us. We were not only planted together in the likeness of Christ's death, but we were also buried with Him and resurrected with Him so that we might walk in newness of life.

This is taught again in Colossians 2:12: "Buried with him in baptism, wherein also ye are risen with him through the faith of the operation of God, who hath raised him from the dead."

The Holy Spirit, in our hearts, makes effective the process of death to the old self-life, the old "I," the old nature. And the Holy Spirit also produces the resurrection life of Christ in us.

Let it be emphasized again that being baptized by the Holy Spirit is not an enduement with power. The baptismal work of the Spirit places us into a position in Christ which makes it possible for us to receive power. Being baptized, however, by the Spirit does not guarantee that power in the life. It does place us in the Body of Christ, which puts us into a position that will enable the power of God to flow through us. Before this last can happen, we have to meet certain responsibilities as believers.

Paul wrote to the Christians in Corinth and in Galatia, all of whom were baptized by the Holy Spirit; many of them, however, were poor examples of the power of the Spirit of Christ. Many were carnal in their attitudes, and others followed false teachings. The filling of the Holy Spirit, or the control of the Holy Spirit, was necessary before the new life in Christ showed up in their experience and walk.

Chapter 5

Sanctification by the Spirit

The subject of sanctification in the Bible is a very important one. Words relating to it and derived from the same basic root words in both Old and New Testaments occur almost 1000 times. These are familiar to us under such words as "sanctify," "sanctification," "holiness," "holy," and even the often misunderstood word "saint."

In its simplest meaning the verb "to sanctify" means "to separate." As this is developed in the Scriptures, we learn that it is used to mean separation to God, or setting apart for God. In being set apart for God the believer is also separated from sinful things. He is separated from the evil ways and thought patterns and behavior of the world. So the idea involves not only being separated to something but also being separated from something. These two prepositions are very important in this connection.

Sanctification also speaks of the course of life befitting those who are separated to God. In other words, sanctification is that relationship with God into which individuals enter by faith in Christ. This is not a human accomplishment but a divine work. Sanctification is one of the great operations of the Holy Spirit in the salvation of believers. Without this work on our behalf there would be no manifes-

47

tation of holy living in our personal conduct. Sanctification, then, is a major aspect of the work of the Holy Spirit on behalf of the Christian.

All believers are sanctified in Christ Jesus. This is why they are called "saints." This means they are sanctified, or holy, ones. Where the word "saint" is used in the New Testament to describe believers, it does not speak of something to which they have attained but to a state into which God in His grace has called them. However, in addition to this, believers are admonished to sanctify themselves so as to live lives consistent with their calling. This is what Paul had reference to when he said in Ephesians 4:4: "I therefore, the prisoner of the Lord, beseech you that ye walk worthy of the vocation wherewith ye are called." The word "sanctify" is not used in this verse, but the thought is inescapable. Our daily lives should show that we are indeed members of God's family.

Sanctification Not Eradication

It is unfortunate that some persons have attributed a meaning to sanctification that the Scriptures do not give it. Some have taught that it means sinlessness, or sinless perfection. By this they mean that inbred sin, or the adamic nature, is eradicated by a special work of the Holy Spirit following salvation.

A study of the Scriptures with regard to sanctification makes the above interpretation untenable. Several different Scripture passages will give an indication of the variety of related meanings connected with the thought of sanctification.

48

In Exodus 40:10,11 Moses wrote concerning the sanctification of objects: "And thou shalt anoint the altar of the burnt-offering, and all his vessels, and sanctify the altar: and it shall be an altar most holy. And thou shalt anoint the laver and his foot, and sanctify it." There was no fallen nature in these inanimate objects; consequently, "sanctification" could not have "eradication" as its root meaning. There is no difficulty, however, when we remember that the verb "to sanctify" means "to separate." Here God was speaking of the separation of certain objects for His service.

In the same Book of Exodus, in Chapter 19, Moses wrote: "And let the priests also, which come near to the Lord, sanctify themselves, lest the Lord break forth upon them" (v. 22). This was a call to persons who served the Lord to set themselves apart to God. This does not say the Holy Spirit was to do it; it was their responsibility. This was a definite choice these men had to make with respect to the work of God. They were to separate themselves from all other callings and separate themselves to the work of the Tabernacle.

The Book of Exodus furnishes us with still another way in which sanctification is used in the Word of God. In Exodus 13:2 we learn: "Sanctify unto me all the firstborn, whatsoever openeth the womb among the children of Israel." Then in Exodus 19:10 we read: "And the Lord said unto Moses, Go unto the people, and sanctify them to day and to morrow, and let them wash their clothes."

According to Exodus 13:2 the firstborn of Israel were to be set apart to God. He claimed them as His. It was the responsibility of their

49

parents and their national leaders to see that this aspect of sanctification was carried out. Then, according to Exodus 19:10, Moses was commanded to sanctify the people. This means they were to be cleansed from all ceremonial and physical defilements and set apart for God so that He could speak to them.

Isaiah the prophet made reference to a very shocking practice among some of the Israelites and used the word "sanctify" in connection with it. He wrote: "They that sanctify themselves, and purify themselves in the gardens behind one tree in the midst, eating swine's flesh, and the abomination, and the mouse, shall be consumed together, saith the Lord" (Isa. 66:17). This is a statement that some persons sanctified themselves to do evil. Instead of separating themselves from evil to God, they were separating themselves from God in order to do sinful things.

In the Gospel of John we learn some things concerning the Father and the Son with regard to the subject of sanctification. We learn first that the Father has sanctified the Son: "Say ye of him, whom the Father hath sanctified, and sent into the world, Thou blasphemest; because I said, I am the Son of God?" (John 10:36).

At a later time the Lord Jesus, in His high-priestly prayer, said, "And for their sakes I sanctify myself, that they also might be sanctified through the truth" (17:19). Surely no one would dare read into these passages the thought that inbred sin was removed from Christ by the Father or by Himself. He had no fallen nature. He was sinless, neither is there any thought here of receiving the Holy Spirit.

Consider still another verse on this matter. In I Corinthians 7:14 Paul said, "For the unbelieving husband is sanctified by the wife, and the unbelieving wife is sanctified by the husband: else were your children unclean; but now are they holy." This rather startling verse tells us that there is an aspect of sanctification applied to unbelievers because of the presence of a believer in the home. This does not teach at all that these unbelievers are saved or that they have received the Holy Spirit. It simply means that because one parent in the home has received Christ as Saviour, that home has a measure of God's blessing, even though only one member of it is a Christian.

What Paul had to say to the Corinthian believers with regard to their sanctification is very instructive for us. He wrote: "Paul, called to be an apostle of Jesus Christ through the will of God, . . . to them that are sanctified in Christ Jesus, called to be saints, with all that in every place call upon the name of Jesus Christ our Lord, both their's and our's" (I Cor. 1:1,2). The word translated "sanctified" and the word translated "saints" come from the same root. So we learn from this that these Corinthian believers were sanctified in Christ through faith. They were set-apart ones.

In spite of this designation in Chapter 1, Paul said in Chapter 3 concerning these same persons, "And I, brethren, could not speak unto you as unto spiritual, but as unto carnal, even as unto babes in Christ. . . . For ye are yet carnal: for whereas there is among you envying, and strife, and divisions, are ye not carnal, and walk as men?"

51

(vv. 1,3). This surely indicates that we must be careful as to what meanings we place on the word "sanctification." These Corinthian believers were sanctified, but their fallen natures were not eradicated. In the purpose of God they were set apart for His glory, though it was not a goal being realized in their daily walk. This was why they were admonished so vigorously by the Apostle Paul.

Still another facet of this truth is brought before us in Hebrews 12:14: "Follow peace with all men, and holiness, without which no man shall see the Lord." This is an admonition not only to follow peace but also to follow holiness. This means we are to follow sanctification, for that is the word in the original. This is not the receiving of the Holy Spirit but a continuous work of the Holy Spirit after He has come into the believer's life.

Peter mentioned still another aspect of this truth. He said in I Peter 3:15: "But sanctify the Lord God in your hearts: and be ready always to give an answer to every man." The idea of sinless perfection or the removing of inbred sin would be an absurdity here. It would be equally illogical to read into this that it means the receiving of the Holy Spirit. What Peter said is to give God first place in our hearts.

The same apostle furnishes us with additional information on the subject of sanctification: "Peter, an apostle of Jesus Christ, to the . . . elect according to the foreknowledge of God the Father, through sanctification of the Spirit, unto obedience and sprinkling of the blood of Jesus Christ" (1:1,2). This verse deals very specifically with persons who are sanctified by the Holy Spirit. This

52

means they are set apart by Him to God the Father and set apart from sin.

A little later in the same chapter Peter said, "But as he which hath called you is holy, so be ye holy in all manner of conversation; because it is written, Be ye holy; for I am holy" (vv. 15,16). The word "holy" in this verse is from the same word that gives us our word "sanctify." So when we put these various verses together from Peter, we learn that it is the responsibility of believers to live holy lives and that this holy living is possible only through the operation of the Holy Spirit in them. Holiness is a characteristic of God, and holiness should mark our Christian walk.

One more passage of Scripture will help round out this phase of our study: "For by one offering he hath perfected for ever them that are sanctified" (Heb. 10:14). In this passage we learn that Jesus Christ, by the sacrifice of His own life, has once and for all sanctified the people of God. He set them apart to God through His death on the cross. Sanctification, then, does not mean sinless perfection, nor does it mean the eradication of our fallen natures. It does mean that God has set us apart to Himself and makes this effective in our lives through the operation of the Holy Spirit.

Three Major Distinctions in Sanctification

The Bible teaches that we are sanctified by the blood of Jesus Christ. This is an *eternal* sanctification. The Bible also teaches that we are sanctified by the Holy Spirit, which is an *internal* sanctification. We also learn that the Holy Spirit sanctifies us through applying the Word to our lives. This has to do with the *external* results of sanctification.

Eternal Sanctification

First of all, then, let us consider eternal sanctification. We read in Hebrews 13:12: "Wherefore Jesus also, that he might sanctify the people with his own blood, suffered without the gate." In Hebrews 10:10 we find: "By the which will we are sanctified through the offering of the body of Jesus Christ once for all." And then in Hebrews 10:29: "Of how much sorer punishment, suppose ye, shall he be thought worthy, who hath trodden under foot the Son of God, and hath counted the blood of the covenant, wherewith he was sanctified, an unholy thing?"

This was a work of sanctification which our Lord Jesus Christ accomplished almost 2000 years ago. By giving His life He made provision for individuals to be set apart from the guilt of sin. This was a potential work for all people but is actual only to those who accept it. Moreover, this was a once-for-all work. It was never to be repeated.

A good illustration familiar to many of us is in Exodus 12. There we are told of the need of the Israelites to slay a lamb and sprinkle its blood on the doorposts of their houses. God had warned that He would come and slay the firstborn in every home in all the land of Egypt. Not even the Israelites could escape this judgment without applying the blood. It was the application of the blood that set them apart from the judgment that was to fall on the land: "For the Lord will pass through to smite the Egyptians; and when he seeth

54

the blood upon the lintel, and on the two side posts, the Lord will pass over the door, and will not suffer the destroyer to come in unto your houses to smite you" (v. 23). To emphasize the matter again, this was sanctification by blood, or being set apart through blood.

Another separation took place at the Red Sea, but this time blood was not required. This was separation by power—God's power in separating Israel from their enemies.

Internal Sanctification

Sanctification is also by the Holy Spirit. This is internal sanctification. This is due to the application in our lives by the Holy Spirit of the work that God has already accomplished for us in Christ. This is a daily experience following the initial receiving of Christ as personal Saviour. This aspect of truth is very clearly set forth in a number of places in the New Testament. Writing to the Corinthians Paul said, "And such were some of you: but ye are washed, but ye are sanctified, but ye are justified in the name of the Lord Jesus, and by the Spirit of our God" (I Cor. 6:11). Their lives had been given over to sin, but that old way of life was reversed through the work of the Lord Jesus Christ and the operation of the Holy Spirit in their daily lives.

To the Thessalonians Paul wrote: "But we are bound to give thanks alway to God for you, brethren beloved of the Lord, because God hath from the beginning chosen you to salvation through sanctification of the Spirit and belief of the truth" (II Thess. 2:13). We also learn from Titus 3:5: "Not by works of righteousness which

55

we have done, but according to his mercy he saved us, by the washing of regeneration, and renewing of the Holy Ghost." The Holy Spirit, then, is responsible for applying the work accomplished by Christ when His blood was shed for us.

A part of the Spirit's responsibilities is to convict us of sin and of righteousness and of judgment. When we turn to Christ, we are placed in such a relationship to God that the threatening judgment is removed. By this we are set apart from the guilt and condemnation of sin. At the same time the Spirit of God produces righteousness in us by His dwelling in us. This is internal sanctification.

External Results

The third aspect of sanctification has to do with the external results. The Bible speaks of our being sanctified by the Word of God as well as by the blood of Christ and by the Holy Spirit.

This makes the believer not of the world, just as Christ is not of the world. God uses His Word under the power and operation of the Holy Spirit to bring about the changes He wants to see in our conduct. Concerning this our Saviour prayed in John 17:16-19: "They are not of the world, even as I am not of the world. Sanctify them through thy truth: thy word is truth. As thou hast sent me into the world, even so have I also sent them into the world. And for their sakes I sanctify myself, that they also might be sanctified through the truth."

This sanctification by the Word of God is a continuous process. It goes on from day to day. There can be no doubt of this in the light of Ephesians 5:26: "That he might sanctify and cleanse it [the Church] with the washing of water by the word."

It is obvious that in order to be set apart by the Word of God we must learn to know the Word of God. One reason why some people are not separated from the old life of sin as they should be, even though they have made a profession of faith in Christ, is not necessarily that they were not born again but that the Word of God does not have the place in their life it should have. The Holy Spirit indwells them, but because they have not taken time in the Word of God and allowed the Holy Spirit to apply it, they have not experienced the purification and cleansing that follows.

That passage of Scripture which reads "Be ye . . . perfect even as your Father which is in heaven is perfect" (Matt. 5:48) has often been misunderstood because we think of the word "perfect" from the standpoint of its modern use and not its biblical use. In this passage the word "perfect" has to do with being mature, or fully developed in a moral sense. We are to be full grown; we are not to remain as babes. This growth comes through sanctification by the Word of God. We are to follow peace and holiness, which shows that there is a process in this development. There is to be the right type of living by us if we are to please God.

If absolute perfection were required in our daily walk, none of us would be able to stand before God. However, in our position before God we are perfect in Christ. This is what gives us our standing before the Heavenly Father. Our daily conduct, on the other hand, is something that

57

should go on to maturity. It is an experience of continuing to grow more and more like Christ. This is accomplished, as we have seen, through the operation of the Holy Spirit and the application of the Word by Him to our daily walk.

Our permanent separation from the body of sin will be realized when our Lord returns. This will be the glorious consummation of our sanctification.

Sanctification—a Crisis or a Process?

We have already considered that a certain aspect of sanctification is a process, but let us investigate this matter further. We will seek to answer the question "Is sanctification a crisis or a process?"

To get to the root of this problem we need to define the meaning of these two words. Webster defines "crisis" as "an unstable or crucial time or state of affairs whose outcome will make a decisive difference for better or worse." This involves a time of decision, a decisive moment, a turning point, a juncture in life. It is a point of time made critical or important by a decision that has to be made.

The word "process," on the other hand, simply means "progress, advance" and refers to "gradual changes that lead toward a particular result." The Word of God makes it plain that there is a crisis as well as a progression with regard to sanctification. It is not "either/or" but "both/and." One has to do with an instantaneous act and the other with a progressive series of actions. Before I can draw a line, I must take my pen or pencil and set it down. That is the point or beginning—a decision, a crisis. It is from that point that the line is drawn.

The decision for holiness, then, is the point. The wholehearted dedication to God is the committal of the whole being. When I commit myself to God, it is by an act of faith. That is the point and the crisis. But then there comes a conformity to the life and character of Christ which becomes and is a process, a gradual continuous matter as long as this present life lasts.

This has a very practical application for us. Are we just praying to God, asking Him to enable us to live a life that pleases Him? Or have we, knowing His will, placed ourselves completely in His hands for Him to do with us as He wishes?

Sanctification as a Crisis

The psalmist sets before us the crisis aspect of sanctification in these words: "Commit thy way unto the Lord; trust also in him; and he shall bring it to pass" (Ps. 37:5). A committal part, trusting is the crisis. By using this word "crisis" we do not mean some great experience but a moment when we make a decision to conform to this life and character of the Lord Jesus Christ since this is the will of God for us. This is an act of appropriating faith. The carrying out of this committal is a process. It takes place in our lives continually. It is gradual and continuous, and as far as this present life is concerned, it is endless—"from faith to faith" (Rom. 1:17).

We learn in Romans 8:28,29: "All things work together for good to them that love God, to them who are the called according to his purpose. For whom he did foreknow, he also did predestinate to be conformed to the image of his Son, that he

59

might be the firstborn among many brethren." The goal of which this process speaks is our conformity to the image of God's Son. Do we want this process to begin in us? To enter into this process is like going through a door. We might call passing through a door a time of crisis or a decision of faith, and on the other side is the path or the process. There has to be a starting point before there can be a continuing experience.

There is not only a crisis with regard to a decision in time, but there must also be an action of faith with regard to that decision. Some people may make a decision yet never act on it. In reality that is no true decision at all. Through faith we act on what we believe. In the words of Romans 6:11-13, we are to reckon ourselves dead to sin but alive to God. Then we are to yield ourselves to God and walk in the Spirit (see Gal. 5:16).

Some persons look for a crisis but never for progress. Some look for an experience yet never come to a point of real decision. Some passages of Scripture will help us with this—passages that point to a moment of time when a decision is made.

For example, II Corinthians 7:1: "Having therefore these promises, dearly beloved, let us cleanse ourselves from all filthiness of the flesh and spirit." In the original language the tense of the word translated "cleanse" indicates a moment of decision. We are to make up our minds, determine and act on this determination to be cleansed from the filthiness of the flesh and the spirit. This is a matter of faith in the sense that we trust God to accomplish this in our lives; but we must decide that this is what we want to do in conformity to the will of God.

60

The closing clause in II Corinthians 7:1 is "perfecting holiness in the fear of God." Here the tense in the original of the word translated "perfecting" speaks of a continuous process. This is something we are to keep on doing.

Another passage illustrating this truth is Ephesians 4:31: "Let all bitterness, and wrath, and anger, and clamour, and evil speaking, be put away from you, with all malice." This verse lists evil habits that have been cultivated as a result of our giving in to our evil natures. These things are to be put from us, as far as our desire and decision is concerned, in a moment, at a definite point in time.

Each of us has an evil nature. This is something inherent in all of us. As a result of this, we have formed evil habits, but we must decide that we do not want to follow them any longer. It is not a matter of reducing them little by little or of putting off one evil thing today and another evil thing tomorrow. It is a decision to be rid of all of them "once for all," just as we might shed a coat.

Familiar to all of us is Hebrews 12:1: "Wherefore seeing we also are compassed about with so great a cloud of witnesses, let us lay aside every weight, and the sin which doth so easily beset us, and let us run with patience the race that is set before us." The words "lay aside" speak of doing something right now. We are not told to pray about some weight or some sin that may be impeding our progress but to reach the personal decision to lay it aside without any reservations about it.

A number of believers write, asking us to pray for them that they might be able to quit some habit. They overlook the fact that in many cases the Bible says each of us is to make a decision to quit these things for ourselves. Now, this is not the whole picture, because such a decision must be made in the power of the Holy Spirit. He will give us the needed grace to make the process following the decision a reality. We are not to lay aside these sins and weights gradually but immediately. Then we will be able to run with patience the race that is set before us. This is progression.

Another verse teaching a definite time of decision is Romans 12:1: "I beseech you therefore, brethren, by the mercies of God, that ye present your bodies a living sacrifice, holy, acceptable unto God, which is your reasonable service." Here the word "present" speaks of something that is to be done in a moment of time. It speaks of something to be done right now. We are to give our bodies over to Him decisively and immediately. It is not a matter of deciding to give an arm today and a leg tomorrow and have God be in control of our ears at some later time. By one decisive act we are to commit our bodies entirely to the Lord. The word "holy" in this passage shows that separation is involved. We are to be separated entirely to God and apart from sin. But this is a decision reached by an act of the will and entered into through faith.

In Hebrews 13:20,21, the writer says, "Now the God of peace, that brought again from the dead our Lord Jesus, that great shepherd of the sheep, through the blood of the everlasting covenant, make you perfect in every good work to do his will, working in you that which is wellpleasing in his sight, through Jesus Christ; to whom be glory for ever and ever." In these two verses we again have the crisis and the process. The first crisis has to do with God's responsibility. God is to make us mature or adjust us so that we follow through on the second aspect, the progressive aspect, and work in us that which is well pleasing in His sight.

How can this be done? Light is thrown on this by Colossians 1:13: "Who hath delivered us from the power of darkness, and hath translated us into the kingdom of his dear Son." This is exactly what happened when you and I were born again. When the Spirit of God came in to make His dwelling in us, He immediately transferred us from the power of darkness and placed us into the kingdom of God's Son. By this means God put us in such a position or place that it was possible for us to do His will. The process follows in the words, "Working in you that which is wellpleasing in his sight" (Heb. 13:21).

In writing to the Thessalonians, Paul said, "And the very God of peace sanctify you wholly; and I pray God your whole spirit and soul and body be preserved blameless unto the coming of our Lord Jesus Christ" (I Thess. 5:23). The phrase "sanctify you wholly" is often misused. The Lord is saying here that He does not just want our spirit or our soul or our body, but that He wants body, soul and spirit—all of us. He wants not merely one part of us but every part of us.

Our responsibility is that of giving ourselves to Him. His responsibility is to take possession and work in us, separating us from sin to holiness and righteousness as He desires. Our part is to present ourselves. God's part is to take us to Himself and set us apart for His purpose and glory. This is true sanctification.

In I Peter 3:15 we are called on to do the sanctifying: "But sanctify the Lord God in your hearts." That simply means that we are to enthrone Christ as Lord. This is not to be done a little at a time but is a decision reached in a moment of time. He is either Lord of all, or He is not Lord at all. We know Him as Jesus, which means "Saviour." We know Him as Christ, which means "the anointed One." But do we know Him as Lord? Is He our Master?

This is not a new person for us to receive but new truth regarding this Person so that we will appropriate Him as Lord and Master and enthrone Him in our lives. This is something we should do once and for all. It is a decision we should make now if we have not made it previously.

Sanctification as a Process

A very clear scripture setting forth sanctification as a process is II Corinthians 3:18: "But we all, with open face beholding as in a glass the glory of the Lord, are changed into the same image from glory to glory, even as by the Spirit of the Lord." This graphically describes the process of sanctification in the power of the Holy Spirit. This is not a program of self-improvement but a divine work that conforms us to the image of Christ. It is a process that leads to change after change in our character to where we become more like Christ with each new step taken. This is spiritual growth and advancement.

The beginning of this process can be a wonderful experience for any of us. I recall keenly the night when I made my decision with regard to consecration. It changed everything in my life. My whole outlook on life and its goals were changed. I determined to prepare for full-time ministry. In this, God was preparing me not only to do but also to be. Through this I came to realize what it meant for Christ to dwell in me and that the life I lived was lived in the faith of the Son of God.

I did not recognize this truth at the time of my salvation. It was sometime after that when these things became apparent to me, and from then on God led me step by step.

Another Scripture passage which throws light on this subject is II Corinthians 4:16: "For which cause we faint not; but though our outward man perish, yet the inward man is renewed day by day." Though time and age take their toll of our physical bodies, the spiritual man is being renewed by the work of the Spirit of God. We grow in grace as this process continues in us. Less and less place is given to the fallen nature and more room is given to Christ. This is possible, however, only as we take time to develop our devotional life through the Word and prayer and submission to the Spirit of God.

According to the 16th chapter of Exodus, when Moses and Aaron introduced Israel to the manna, they said of it, "And in the morning, then ye shall see the glory of the Lord" (v. 7). The lesson for us here is that just as Israel had to gather the manna day by day, so we gather the manna of God's Word day by day. In this way we are constantly refreshed spiritually and inwardly renewed.

The Apostle Paul said in Colossians 1:11, "Strengthened with all might, according to his glorious power, unto all patience and longsuffering

65

with joyfulness." This being strengthened with all might is not the result of one tremendous experience but of a continuous experience. Our spiritual strength is increased as we devote ourselves more and more to the Lord.

In His conversation with the woman at the well our Saviour said, "But whosoever drinketh of the water that I shall give him shall never thirst; but the water that I shall give him shall be in him a well of water springing up into everlasting life" (John 4:14). The Saviour was saying that not only would He give new life to those who wished it, but this life would be replenished day by day. It was to be like a fountain pouring out its refreshing waters without interruption.

We know that everlasting life is given to us the moment we believe; but it is also a kind of life which is manifested more and more as we walk with the Lord.

Still another passage dealing with the process of sanctification is II Peter 1:3: "According as his divine power hath given unto us all things that pertain unto life and godliness." The word "life" here may refer to the crisis, for it is dealing with eternal life. Godliness has to do with process—that which is seen in the daily walk. There is to be a constant daily flow of spiritual power.

In the words of Ephesians 6:10 we are to "be strong in the Lord, and in the power of His might." This speaks of our being constantly and continually strengthened in the Lord.

The Apostle John touches on this subject from another angle. He says in I John 3:3, "And every man that hath this hope in him purifieth himself, even as he is pure." The hope spoken of here is the

66

coming of the Lord. In the light of this hope we enter, through the process of daily purification, into the likeness of Christ's purity. This will be climaxed when Christ comes. Then we shall be changed completely to be like Him.

We are cleansed instantaneously from the guilt of sin, but there is the constant action of purifying us from the power of sin from that time on. There is defilement by sin in our daily lives, and from that we must be daily purified.

This is illustrated for us in the 13th chapter of John's Gospel, where we read how Jesus washed the disciples' feet. He came to Peter, but Peter did not want the Lord to wash his feet. Our Saviour answered him: "He that is washed needeth not save to wash his feet, but is clean every whit: and ye are clean, but not all" (v. 10). What the Lord was saying was that once we have been regenerated, we have been cleansed once and for all from the guilt of sin. But daily defilement calls for daily cleansing, of which foot washing was an illustration.

It is very much like a woman who does her spring housecleaning or redecorates her house. Once such work is done, she does not leave it as though it needed no further touch. Perhaps daily, certainly every week, depending on the condition of things, the housecleaning is kept up. This is what the Lord is talking about here with regard to the daily cleansing in the Christian's life.

Peter learned this truth well, for he later wrote: "But grow in grace, and in the knowledge of our Lord and Saviour Jesus Christ. To him be glory both now and for ever" (II Pet. 3:18). The command is not to grow *into* grace but *in* grace and in the knowledge of our Lord. Again this speaks of something that is progressive. It is dealing with spiritual development.

In Hebrews 10:14 we read: "For by one offering he hath perfected for ever them that are sanctified." A more accurate translation would be, "For by one offering he hath perfected for ever them that are being sanctified." His one offering perfects forever—once for all—His people. We are sanctified through the offering of the body of Jesus Christ once for all, Hebrews 10:10 says. This is instantaneous sanctification. But there is also the progressive aspect of sanctification dealt with in Hebrews 10:14. We are being sanctified, and this leads to maturity and godliness.

Israel passed through the Jordan, which was a crisis; but it took them five years to conquer Canaan, which was a process. We have already seen in Romans 12:1 that we are to yield ourselves once for all to God. This is a crisis. The second verse of this chapter says, "Be not conformed to this world: but be ye transformed by the renewing of your mind, that ye may prove what is that good, and acceptable, and perfect, will of God." Here we are faced with a process of transformation with regard to our character.

Is this crisis experience ever to be repeated? I would say that if it is an act of restoration, yes, it should be. But let me qualify that statement. When we backslide, we do not need to go through the whole matter again. What we need to do is to acknowledge that there was a previous dedication and then confess our failure before the Lord. First John 1:9 simply says, "If we confess our sins [agree with God that we are sinful], he is faithful and just to forgive us our sins, and to cleanse us from all unrighteousness." So then we, in a sense, rededicate ourselves to the Lord by an act of the will. Another expression for this is "to repent." In Revelation 2:4,5 we read that the Lord said to the church in Ephesus: "Nevertheless I have somewhat against thee, because thou hast left thy first love. Remember therefore from whence thou art fallen, and repent, and do the first works." He did not say that they had to begin all over from the first but that they were to remember from what they had fallen.

We must maintain an attitude of consecration. When this is not maintained, when that "line" is broken that was begun at a certain crisis point, then we must return to the place in the line where the process of development was broken. We start again where we stopped.

We may also speak of the confirming or renewal of our attitude of committal to the Lord as a crisis. When we do this we are saying "amen" to what has already taken place.

Concerning this, Lamentations 3:21-23 says, "This I recall to my mind, therefore have I hope. It is of the Lord's mercies that we are not consumed, because his compassions fail not. They are new every morning: great is thy faithfulness." The Lord does not cast us off forever when we make a crisis decision and then have failed to carry through. Though He is grieved by our failure, still He has compassion and does not take pleasure when He has to afflict or grieve us. What He desires is that we turn back to Him again.

Chapter 6

Filled With the Spirit

According to Ephesians 5:18 the Christian should be filled with the Spirit. Here are the exact words: "And be not drunk with wine, wherein is excess; but be filled with the Spirit." This aspect of the work of the Holy Spirit is experiential; that is, it has to do with our everyday experience, our daily walk as Christians. Such aspects of the Holy Spirit's work as the baptism and sealing are not on the level of our consciousness. They are objective facts. They are realities but are outside the realm of our everyday experience. Even regeneration, though it relates to our experience, was the work of a moment. It is true not because we felt different or passed through some great emotional upheaval but because the Word of God tells us it took place the moment we believed.

The filling of the Holy Spirit has to do with the activity of the new-found spiritual life within us. This is not the release of new physical energy but spiritual power that operates within us, with the Holy Spirit as the source. The filling of the Spirit is essential for spiritual growth. Without this aspect of the Spirit's work we could not go on to maturity in the Christian life.

A Definition

We will be helped in our understanding of this work of the Spirit if we carefully define what is meant by being filled. One Greek lexicon gives this definition concerning the word translated "filled" in Ephesians 5:18: "To pervade, ... to influence fully, possess fully." For a believer to be "filled with the Holy Spirit," then, means that the Holy Spirit possesses his mind and heart—his very being.

A good illustration of what the Bible means by being "filled" is found in Luke 5:26. The Saviour had just healed a paralytic, and the people who saw the miracle glorified God and "were filled with fear." That means they were controlled by fear. Fear possessed them, and their attitudes and actions were affected by that fear. So then, when the believer is filled with the Spirit, it means that the Holy Spirit controls the mind, the heart and the body of the Christian.

A contrast concerning controlling power is given in the scripture with which we began this chapter: "Be not drunk with wine, wherein is excess; but be filled with the Spirit" (Eph. 5:18). The first part is a warning not to be controlled by wine. The control that alcoholic beverages have over individuals is a problem of national proportion today. The result of such control is never good. The person controlled by alcohol is under a power greater than his own.

It is equally true that when the Christian is controlled by the Holy Spirit, he is controlled by a power greater than his own. It is just such power that is needed to break the hold on our lives of the flesh, which is the self-life. When the self-life is in control, we have carnality; when the Holy Spirit is in control we have spirituality. A Christian is either carnal or spiritual, depending on who or what controls him.

A Continuous Action

The expression "be filled with the Spirit" is a command that might be translated "keep on being filled with the Holy Spirit." Continuous action is involved in the force of these words. It denotes an experience that ought not to be intermittent but continuous.

It is clear from the New Testament that being filled with the Spirit was a repeated experience on the part of believers. According to Acts 2:4, when the Holy Spirit came at Pentecost, the believers were filled with the Spirit. Then in Acts 4:31 we learn how the believers were again filled with the Spirit. The apostles had been imprisoned for preaching the gospel, then released. Instead of obeying the threats of the Jewish leaders, God's servants prayed for boldness to keep on preaching the Word. Then they were filled with the Spirit.

The baptism by the Spirit, on the other hand, was a once-for-all act. This is not something that is done again and again. It takes place only once.

On the other hand, Ephesians 5:18 could be translated "be being filled" meaning that control by the Holy Spirit should be a moment-by-moment matter. It is not a once-for-all act but a continuing experience.

Light is thrown on this in Galatians 5:16, where the word "fill" is not used but the admonition is "Walk in the Spirit, and ye shall not fulfil the lust of the flesh." This is just another way of telling us to allow the Holy Spirit to control us, and the desires of the flesh nature will be overcome by the desires of the Spirit of God.

The same truth is given in Romans 8:4: "That the righteousness of the law might be fulfilled in us, who walk not after the flesh, but after the Spirit." Here again the thought is our being under the control of the Spirit instead of being controlled by the flesh. The passage goes on to say: "For they that are after the flesh [under the control of the flesh] do mind the things of the flesh [their minds are occupied with the things of the self-life]; but they that are after the Spirit [controlled by the Spirit] the things of the Spirit. For to be carnally minded is death; but to be spiritually minded is life and peace. Because the carnal mind is enmity against God: for it is not subject to the law of God, neither indeed can be. So then they that are in the flesh cannot please God" (vv. 5-8).

The person who has the Spirit of God dwelling in him is not in the flesh but in the Spirit. On the other hand, if a person does not have the Spirit of Christ, he does not belong to Christ. The Spirit of God indwells the believer to give him life and then to control his daily walk.

We should not think of the Holy Spirit's filling in the sense that we would think of water filling a bottle. The Christian is not a receptacle to be emptied in order to be filled. Neither is the Holy Spirit a substance that fills a receptacle. I take my car to a filling station and say to the attendant, "Fill it up." But that is not the way I can speak with the Lord concerning my life. I cannot say to

Him, "Lord, fill it up," as though I had used up the Holy Spirit and needed more of Him.

Total Control

No, the Holy Spirit is a Person, a holy Person who indwells us in order to control us. To be totally filled by the Spirit means to be totally controlled by Him.

We may have a temporary guest in our home, and though we would hope he would feel at home, we would not expect him to rearrange the furniture any way he preferred in the room we give him. On the other hand, if we had a permanent boarder, the case would be different. He could move the furniture in his room to where it best suited him.

However, in talking about total control, we can think of our lives as being made up of many rooms and turning over every room in the house to the Holy Spirit. There is the financial room and the pleasure room and all of the other rooms that make up life. All of these should be turned over to the direction and leadership of the Spirit of God. The Holy Spirit does not take control of our lives automatically the moment we believe. It is true that He regenerates us and baptizes us into the Body of Christ and seals us. But if He is to control our daily experience, it is done only with our permission and having the right attitude toward His direction. Though we receive Christ as personal Saviour, the Holy Spirit does not control us until we recognize that He is a member of the Godhead, indwelling us for the purpose of directing our lives. When we show complete confidence in His control and turn over everything to Him by an act of the will, then we are filled, or controlled, by Him.

At times we are surprised to learn that though we believed we had turned everything over to the direction of the Holy Spirit, there are still areas in our lives from which He has been shut out. These He brings to our attention. Each time this is done it calls for a fresh relinquishing of our control and the reestablishing of His control in this aspect of our lives as well.

To be under the control of the Spirit of God does not mean a spasmodic filling—for example, for a preacher when he has to bring a message or a Sunday school teacher who has to teach a class. This is not filling for some particular great event but a moment-by-moment control by the Spirit of God. There is no victory possible in our lives unless the Spirit of God is given first place in our hearts.

An additional fact concerning Ephesians 5:18 is that it is addressed not to a chosen few, such as Christian workers, but to all believers. It makes no difference what position we may fill in secular life or in Christian leadership, we are to be controlled by the Spirit at all times. The work we do is to be under His direction.

Still another truth to observe is that the verb is in the passive voice, which means that the subject of the verb is being acted upon. We are the subject of the verb in this case. We do not control the Holy Spirit, but He controls us. This is not the work of man but the work of God upon man. Being controlled by the Spirit is not the result of our tears or praying or agonizing. We are acted upon by the Holy Spirit when we submit to Him.

This filling of the Spirit is a repeated experience. This is a blessing, for if it were limited to a once-only experience, sin being what it is, we would be in despair. It is easy for us to lapse into submission to the self-life. We need to confess this and again renew our surrender to the Spirit of God.

Why Be Under the Spirit's Control?

Why does God want to exercise His control over our lives? In the first place, Christ needs to live again on earth through us. That is the only way He can do His work in the world at present. This is possible only when we are under the complete control of the Holy Spirit. He forms Christ in us and lives out Christ's life through us.

This great fact is seen in what we call the "body truths" in the New Testament. Christ is the head of the mystical Body, of which believers are members. They are baptized into it by the Holy Spirit. The life we exercise as members of this Body is the life of Christ; therefore, it is necessary that the Spirit of God control us so that this life can be expressed through us.

We also need to be filled, or controlled, for our testimony's sake. We can speak words, but they do not do the work that God intends them to do unless the Spirit of God uses them. The same is true of our prayer life. We can go through the motions of prayer, but unless the Spirit of God is energizing us and directing us, our prayers are empty. The Word of God instructs us to pray "in the Spirit," and so His control is needed for that also.

Another factor to consider is that God has a purpose for every believer. This can be realized only as we see what place God has for us and allow

Him to enable us to meet the requirements that purpose calls for. The Holy Spirit is responsible for directing the total work of God on the earth. Whether it is in the homeland or on the mission field, regardless of what country is involved, the Holy Spirit coordinates all of the ministry. So then, if every individual Christian would be under the Spirit's total control, the work that He wants done in the evangelizing of the world would be done in this generation.

As we have noted before, the new birth is a supernatural work performed by the Holy Spirit within us, but the new birth marks only the beginning of the Christian life. We were born into the family as babes in order that we might grow to maturity. For this the control of the Spirit of God is needed. This is the goal of God in our lives, according to I Thessalonians 5:23: "And the very God of peace sanctify you wholly; and I pray God that your whole spirit and soul and body be preserved blameless unto the coming of our Lord Jesus Christ." God has set us apart to Himself so that this goal of righteousness might be realized in us.

The spirit, soul and body are all spoken of here. The soul is the seat of the mind, and none of us would surely dispute that our minds need to be under the direct control of the Spirit of God. What do we think about? What do we think about when we are not in church or reading our Bible? What do we think about when we see a rack of modern magazines? It is necessary that the Spirit of God control our thought life or our thoughts will veer in the wrong direction. We are told, "Let this mind be in you, which was also in Christ Jesus" (Phil. 2:5).

The soul is also the seat of the emotions. These, too, need to be God directed. What stirs them up, and what methods do we employ to bring tranquillity?

Then there is our conscience. It is popular to speak of the conscience as being a guide, but where does it guide us? We need the Spirit of God to direct the conscience; otherwise we can be led astray. For a guide to the conscience the Lord uses the Word. Through the Word the Spirit of God instructs us.

The soul is also the seat of the will. Decisions must be made constantly. But what decisions we make will depend on who is in control of our lives.

Then there is our body to be considered. We have five senses, and all of these senses need to be directed in the proper channels. The Spirit of God needs to be our "Divine Censor." What do we see? What do we look at? We need the Spirit of God to help us see the right things and listen for the right things. Some people become drunk with wine because they have acquired a perverted taste. The Spirit of God must control us in this direction also. To be controlled by wine instead of by the Spirit spells sin and trouble. Remember that as long as we are under the control of the Spirit, we do not fulfill the desires of the flesh.

Conditions for the Filling of the Holy Spirit

Do the Scriptures teach that we must wait on the Lord in order to be filled with the Spirit? In other words, is waiting one of the conditions required for the filling?

Consider first of all what is said of our Saviour in Acts 1:4,5: "And, being assembled together with them, commanded them that they should not depart from Jerusalem, but wait for the promise of the Father, which, saith he, ye have heard of me. For John truly baptized with water; but ye shall be baptized with the Holy Ghost not many days hence." This was a direct command by our Saviour to the disciples to wait. They were to wait in order to be baptized in the Holy Spirit.

Wait for What?

Now consider Acts 2, beginning with verse 1: "And when the day of Pentecost was fully come, they were all with one accord in one place. And suddenly there came a sound from heaven as of a rushing mighty wind, and it filled all the house where they were sitting. And there appeared unto them cloven tongues like as of fire, and it sat upon each of them. And they were all filled with the Holy Ghost, and began to speak with other tongues, as the Spirit gave them utterance" (vv. 1-4). In the passage in Acts 1 we saw that the disciples were instructed to wait for the baptism in the Holy Spirit. Here we are told that when the Holy Spirit came, they were filled, or controlled, by Him. Does this latter passage lay down the principle that believers must wait and pray before they can be filled with the Spirit?

The coming of the Holy Spirit at Pentecost was preordained, just as was the coming of the Lord Jesus Christ into the world. When the time was

79

fully come, our Lord was born. And so it was with regard to the coming of the Holy Spirit. According to the typology of the Old Testament, He was to come on the Day of Pentecost, which was 50 days after the Passover. The specific Pentecost at which the Holy Spirit would come was predicted by our Lord Himself. After having been with His disciples 40 days following His resurrection, He left them with the injunction to wait in Jerusalem until the Holy Spirit came. They waited for ten days, and the Spirit came. The question still persists: Did they wait for the baptism of the Holy Spirit or for the filling of the Holy Spirit?

In Chapter 4 we learned that the Greek word translated "baptize" means "to submerge" or "to overwhelm." It means introducing or placing a person or thing into a new environment or into union with something else so as to alter its condition or its relationship to its previous environment or condition. Through His baptismal work the Holy Spirit placed the Christians into the Body of Jesus Christ. This was what they were to wait for. This was foundational to the other works the Holy Spirit was to perform. We must carefully distinguish between the baptism and the filling or we will be confused in our thinking and our teaching.

The instruction the Saviour gave the disciples was to wait for the baptism of the Holy Spirit. It is through that baptism that the believer is brought into vital union with Christ. It is not a work necessary for power but for placing the believer into the Body of Christ so that there can be power. It is true that as far as a time in history is concerned, the Holy Spirit came at Pentecost to take up His eternal residence in believers of this age. This was the beginning of His forming of the Body of Christ. This is foundational to all the other works of the Spirit within us that will be considered later.

There is not one single command, nor is there one single example in the whole New Testament, where believers are told to wait for the filling of the Holy Spirit. It was while they were in the upper room that the Holy Spirit came upon the disciples. Through prayer and obedience to the Saviour's command they were prepared for the Holy Spirit's coming. His coming itself was preordained according to God's sovereign purpose. This was a specified time—the Day of Pentecost; it was a specified place—the city of Jerusalem; and it was for a specific purpose—the baptism in the Spirit.

We must not overlook the fact, however, that not only were the believers baptized into the Body of Christ on the Day of Pentecost, they were also filled with the Holy Spirit at that time. They were told to wait for the baptism, but God gave them the filling in addition. Too many of us who have known what it is to trust in Jesus Christ as our personal Saviour have been satisfied with merely having the guilt of sin removed. We have acted as though being born of the Spirit was the end of God's work in us and for us. We have seen that this is not the case. The moment we were born again we were also baptized into the Body of Christ. This does not mean that we were automatically filled or controlled by the Holy Spirit as far as His leading and directing us in the Christian life is concerned. This is why it is very important that we consider the matter of the Holy Spirit's filling. This must also be noted: Though God nowhere tells believers to tarry or to pray for the filling, this does not mean that the filling is given without any kind of condition.

Obedience

There are conditions, and the basic condition is obedience. We would not say that prayer is not involved in this, but "tarrying prayer," waiting in prayer for the filling, is not the primary prerequisite. Obedience is the prerequisite.

A familiar passage to us is Romans 12:1, where we are told to present our bodies "a living sacrifice, holy, acceptable unto God." In obedience to this we are to present or yield ourselves to God. God wants our bodies so that He can control us through the power of the Holy Spirit.

The Holy Spirit indwells us the moment we trust in Christ, but he controls us only as we surrender to Him. This is why Paul wrote such a verse as Romans 6:13: "Neither yield ye your members as instruments of unrighteousness unto sin: but yield yourselves unto God, as those that are alive from the dead [made alive by the Spirit], and your members as instruments of righteousness unto God."

In the same chapter and verse 16 the apostle wrote: "Know ye not, that to whom ye yield yourselves servants to obey, his servants ye are to whom ye obey; whether of sin unto death, or of obedience unto righteousness?" We must obey God and yield to the Holy Spirit so that we might be filled by Him, thereby allowing Him, through His absolute control of our lives, to produce righteous acts in us.

The basic work for this had already been done, according to verse 22: "But now being made free from [the power of] sin, and become servants to God, ye have your fruit unto holiness, and the end everlasting life." The groundwork has been laid for us to produce a holy life, but what is needed is our submission to, and cooperation with, the Holy Spirit.

Thirsting and Trusting

Together with yielding there must be a desire to be filled and then the act of obedience whereby we appropriate the filling. Our Lord said, "If any man thirst, let him come unto me, and drink. He that believeth on me, as the scripture hath said, out of his belly shall flow rivers of living water. (But this spake he of the Spirit, which they that believe on him should receive: for the Holy Ghost was not yet given; because that Jesus was not yet glorified)" (John 7:37-39).

Here, then, are two prerequisites for the filling of the Holy Spirit. First there is thirst—a thirst for the Spirit of God to take control of us. Then we are to trust the Lord Jesus for the Spirit's control. "If any man thirst, let him come unto me, and drink" (v. 37). Thirst suggests desire, and drinking suggests obedience and trust.

In this desire to be filled with the Holy Spirit must be included our wanting God to judge and put away sin in our lives. We must have the desire to be separated to the Lord and from the world's ties and systems of evil. We must want to see effective in our lives the fact that we are dead to sin and alive to God. This is true positionally, but it can be made true in our walk on the earth only as we yield to the Holy Spirit's control.

It also means that there must be a desire for the fruit of the Spirit in our lives. Do we want love, joy, peace and the other evidences of the Spirit's life in us? Do we long to enthrone Christ as Lord?

When this desire moves us to trust, then we drink or taste. In the words of our Saviour, out of our innermost beings "shall flow rivers of living water" (v. 38). We not only trust Christ to save us from sin, but we trust Him to fill us with the Spirit. This particular phase of believing or trusting in Christ is a continuous trusting, a continuous committing of ourselves to the Lord in order to be controlled by the Holy Spirit. This is a momentary, hourly and daily matter.

When we sin, it means that the self-life has taken control. We must confess that sin and be cleansed and restored to fellowship. The Lord is faithful if we confess our sins and is just to forgive us our sins and to cleanse us from all unrighteousness (I John 1:9). The Lord not only forgives us but cleanses us, thus making room for the Holy Spirit to again take complete possession of our lives.

Whereas the new birth and being baptized by the Holy Spirit into the Body of Christ are once-for-all acts, being filled with the Holy Spirit is something we must deal with constantly. There must be a constant desire for His control, a continuous yielding to the Holy Spirit, all of which involves the forsaking of sin and the seeking of righteousness. This speaks of a continuous daily devotional habit of life.

I believe that it is possible for a deeper under-standing of this control to exist as we gain deeper insights into the knowledge of Christ. This is un-doubtedly what Paul meant when he said, "That I may know him [Christ], and the power of his res-urrection" (Phil. 3:10). This knowing is a contin-uous process. Paul laid no claims to having reached complete attainment in this, but he set the control of the Holy Spirit in his life as his goal. If a man like Paul had to admit that he was not absolutely under the control of the Spirit at all times, how much more we need to give ourselves constantly to the Lord for His filling, or control!

A Crisis and a Process in the Spirit's Control

It is necessary for us to look once again at Romans 12:1,2. The crisis and the process with regard to the filling of the Holy Spirit are brought before us in these two verses: "I beseech you there-fore, brethren, by the mercies of God, that ye pre-sent your bodies a living sacrifice, holy, acceptable unto God, which is your reasonable service. And be not conformed to this world: but be ye trans-formed by the renewing of your mind, that ye may prove what is that good, and acceptable, and per-fect, will of God."

The first word to consider is the word "pre-sent." This verb in the original signifies an act that is to be done once and for all. We are to present our bodies—which involves the entire life, every phase of our being—for all time to the Lord.

This is not a call to a dedication to do some particular ministry but a dedication of the entire person to the control of the Holy Spirit. Some

Christians speak of having dedicated their lives to be missionaries or to some particular phase of Christian service, but that is not the primary emphasis here. What is being considered is the presenting or yielding of our entire being to the Lord's control. If He wants to assign us to some specific aspect of Christian work, that is all very well, but that will follow after we have yielded ourselves to His control.

The question Paul is raising has to do with who will run our lives. Will it be Christ through the Holy Spirit, or will it be the self-life? Who is going to be in charge? God is not asking us to drop off sin a little at a time but to turn over our entire life to Him.

The next expression to note is "Be not conformed." This has to do with separation and flows from the presenting or the yielding of the body to Christ. We belong to the Lord; we have been purchased by Him. We are indwelt by the Holy Spirit. Nothing could be more wonderful than being His temple.

The third expression is "be ye transformed." This transformation is also an act, a continuous one, flowing from our having yielded. This is a transformation that centers in the mind. This kind of mind in us causes us to follow with obedience the direction of the Holy Spirit. This is the force of Romans 8:5: "They that are after the flesh [controlled by the flesh nature] do mind the things of the flesh; but they that are after the Spirit [controlled by the Spirit of God] the things of the Spirit."

This gives proper direction to the life. On the one hand we are not to be conformed to the world;

on the other hand, we are to be transformed by the renewing of our minds. Through this we prove what is that good and acceptable and perfect will of God. The word "prove" in this case means "discern" or "test" or "know." So there is even progress in knowing the will of God. This speaks of growth. This, however, begins with the presenting of ourselves, or yielding of ourselves, to the Lord and then continues as a process from day to day. There is the once-for-all act, then the separation and the transformation and the knowing of the will of God—all in this sequence. Without the filling of the Holy Spirit, of course, this goal would never be realized. We need divine power to reach this divine goal.

Hindrances to the Filling

The Word not only tells us of a crisis and a process with regard to the filling of the Holy Spirit, but it also shows us what things interfere with the filling of the Holy Spirit. In dealing with these matters we are not contradicting the fact that the Holy Spirit indwells the believer forever. In touching on these negative things we are showing what comes between us and the Holy Spirit's controlling us.

We read in Ephesians 4:30: "And grieve not the holy Spirit of God, whereby ye are sealed unto the day of redemption." Through the Spirit we are sealed unto the day of redemption, yet we are warned not to grieve Him. This is a most solemn admonition. The same portion of Scripture goes on to show that we grieve Him when we sin. Sin does not break off the Spirit's indwelling us, but it does affect our relationship as far as His fellowship and

87

control is concerned. Though we do not lose the presence of the Holy Spirit, we do lose His direction in our lives.

Some of the sins that grieve Him are bitterness, wrath, anger, clamor and evil speaking, which is another expression for gossip. Malice is also added to the list.

On the positive side, we are to be kind one to another, tenderhearted, forgiving one another (Eph. 4:32). In Ephesians 5:4 we are admonished: "Neither filthiness, nor foolish talking, nor jesting, which are not convenient: but rather giving of thanks." In place of these evil things we are to give thanks.

Another obstacle to the filling of the Holy Spirit is our quenching of the Spirit. This word speaks of disobedience to His direction. When He moves within our soul to do something and we do not obey, we quench Him. This is a sin of omission rather than a sin of commission. It is just as wrong, however, to not do something the Holy Spirit wants us to do as it is to do something He has told us not to do. He takes control of our lives in order that He might produce a life measured by the standards of God's holiness. For this reason, then, we must give ourselves entirely to Him and not grieve Him or quench Him.

When sin is found in the life, we must employ God's method of dealing with it. According to Romans 6 and many other portions, it is not God's will that we should sin. The Lord has not only provided forgiveness from sin's guilt but also deliverance from its power. He tells us that we are dead to sin; therefore we should no longer live in sin.

Only the Holy Spirit, of course, can make this true in our experience.

In Romans 6 Paul gave the doctrinal aspects of this way of victory and said in verse 6 that we know the "old man is crucified" with Christ. My whole self has been crucified with the Lord Jesus Christ, but I must depend on the Holy Spirit to make this a reality in my experience.

We are to reckon on this, and the word "reckon" means "to accept something as certain." It is not enough to say to God that we know this truth; we must count it true in our daily walk. We need to constantly rest in the power of the Spirit to overcome the sin nature in the life. Only the Spirit can make effective the fact that the believer has died with Christ.

When we do sin, according to the 12th chapter of Hebrews, there will be chastening. The purpose of chastening is for our profit—that we might be partakers of God's holiness. Chastening does not always mean judgment or punishment for sin; rather, it is a disciplinary action on God's part which He employs to break the hold of the adamic nature on our lives.

The Lord allows certain things to happen in our lives in order to train us to avoid evil and to seek the good. He chastens us in order to free us from the wrong direction we may be following.

Before there can be cleansing, there must be confession of the sin. This is the teaching of I John 1:9: "If we confess our sins, he is faithful and just to forgive us our sins, and to cleanse us from all unrighteousness." We are to agree with Him that there is a certain sin in our life, and we are to condemn it as He had condemned it. There will be no victory over that sin if we seek to avoid the convicting work of the Holy Spirit with regard to it. So let us agree with Him when He convicts us of wrong, and He will forgive us and cleanse us.

What Is a Spirit-Filled Person Like?

First of all, a Spirit-filled person is dependent on the Holy Spirit for the continuous manifestation of his spiritual life. Paul wrote in Galatians 5:16: "This I say then, Walk in the Spirit, and ye shall not fulfil the lust of the flesh." This describes the Christian life as a walk in a certain environment and toward a certain goal. In walking physically we must take successive steps. As we walk, one foot supports the body while the other foot moves forward. Translate this into the spiritual life and we find it is lived one step at a time, each step being taken in faith in God.

To walk in the Spirit means we place confidence in the Holy Spirit to uphold us as we step forward with Christ. We are confident in this kind of walk that the Spirit will empower us to live so as not to be ruled by the flesh but rather by the Spirit Himself.

We need to depend constantly on the Spirit to help us because of the high standards required in the Christian life. These are all gathered together for us in one brief verse in which the writer to the Hebrews says, "That we might be partakers of his [God's] holiness" (12:10). This standard of holiness calls for a higher quality of life than man would demand or even think of.

This standard of holiness covers every aspect of

life. For example, the Lord Jesus said, "A new commandment I give unto you, That ye love one another; as I have loved you, that ye also love one another" (John 13:34). Can we meet this standard by ourselves? Is it possible for us to love other persons as Christ has loved us? This is, humanly speaking, impossible. How can we love those who may revile us or say evil things about us behind our backs? How can we naturally love persons who are hateful in their attitude toward us and treat us with contempt? Yet this is what is expected of us.

Not only is it expected, but it is commanded of us. Such a standard can be met only as we recognize the fact that we belong to Christ and that the Holy Spirit dwells in us. Romans 5:5 says, "Because the love of God is shed abroad in our hearts by the Holy Ghost which is given unto us." Such love is possible in us when we are under the control of the Holy Spirit. When He fills us, He is able to produce this kind of life in us. This is the only way we can possibly fulfill the command to love unloving neighbors, not only as ourselves but as Jesus has loved us.

The Thought Life

We must depend on the Spirit's power to control our thought life. Here is what the Scriptures have to say on that point: "The weapons of our warfare are not carnal, but mighty through God [the work of the Holy Spirit in us], . . . bringing into captivity every thought to the obedience of Christ" (II Cor. 10:4,5). Only the Spirit of God can make this possible in our lives, and He does this only when we are under His complete control.

91

When an evil thought comes, what are we to do? We should turn it over to the Spirit and ask Him to take charge. I have personally tried this for years. It is the only method that works for me. I cannot help it when a thought comes, whether it is good or bad, because the Devil is around shooting his darts at us. We do not, however, have to harbor these thoughts. So the moment a wrong thought comes, I ask the Holy Spirit to take over and deliver me, for that is His responsibility. When I give Him control, He gives me the victory. I have experienced this thousands of times.

Consider the subject of prayer. In I Thessalonians 5:17 we are told to pray without ceasing. Can we possibly do that? There is only one way it can be done, and that is through letting the Holy Spirit control us. As He dwells in us and we continue to give Him control so that no sin hinders His working in our hearts, He reminds us of the things He wants us to pray about.

In my own experience I have found that when I am wakeful at night and a certain person comes to mind, I ask the direction of the Holy Spirit in praying for that person. I may not know any specific need that person has, but I have received letters in which the person has told me how God at a certain time did something special in his life. This certain time coincided with the burden the Lord had laid on my heart.

Thankful

Another admonition is found in I Thessalonians 5:18 and is impossible for us to fulfill without the help of the Holy Spirit. It says, "In every thing give thanks."

This means to give thanks even in the most difficult situations in life. Suppose, for example, we suffer a car accident and our automobile is badly damaged; could we give thanks? On top of that, suppose the other fellow was responsible and was unable to meet his obligation; could we still be thankful?

Some time ago a young lad ran his car into the back of mine. He did not have a penny of insurance. The damage was not small. At first I thought this was going to be bad, but then I remembered that the Lord's hand was on my life, so I prayed for His wisdom to know why He let this happen. He immediately spoke to my heart that this was to be used as a spiritual contact with regard to this young man's salvation. The accident gave me the opportunity of presenting Christ to him and to the others who were in the car with him. The Lord even took care of the cost of the accident, for though the young man was without money then, he paid the bill a little at a time as he was able.

A Threefold Enemy

We are dependent on the Holy Spirit's help because of the power of our Enemy. We face a threefold enemy—the world, the flesh and the Devil.

Consider the flesh nature, for example. According to Romans 7:18, there is no good thing in our fallen natures. Paul found himself with a real conflict on his hands. He was a believer, but the things he wanted to do to please God he found he did not do, and the things that displeased God he found

93

himself doing. He discovered the way of victory was through the Lord Jesus Christ and the presence and control of the indwelling Spirit.

Satan is another enemy over whom we have no power in ourselves. Peter, however, told how this archenemy of ours can be overcome: "Humble yourselves therefore under the mighty hand of God, that he may exalt you in due time: casting all your care upon him; for he careth for you. Be sober, be vigilant; because your adversary the devil, as a roaring lion, walketh about, seeking whom he may devour: whom resist stedfast in the faith" (I Pet. 5:6-9). The way of victory is through faith in the Holy Spirit, who lives within us.

The third enemy is the world, concerning which James says, "Ye adulterers and adulteresses, know ye not that the friendship of the world is enmity with God? Whosoever therefore will be a friend of the world is the enemy of God" (James 4:4). The real victory over the world was provided through Christ's sacrifice for us on Calvary. By it the world was crucified to us and we to the world (Gal. 6:14). This is made applicable to us through the work of the Holy Spirit within. The victory that overcomes the world is our faith (I John 5:4). So once more we see why the control of the Holy Spirit over us in a complete way is absolutely essential for our victory.

It is necessary, then, for us to cooperate with the Holy Spirit in this matter of His control of us. He is a Person, and He indwells us for the purpose of controlling us. It is not believers using the power of God for victory in service but rather God the Holy Spirit, by His power, using believers.

We need to get this matter clear and straight in our minds. The Christian life is not merely letting go and letting God, as some have said. It is more than that. To many persons, to let go and let God is simply to say, "Lord, you go ahead, and I will just forget about it." We have a responsibility to meet. We must take hold with God. It is not mere submission to the will of God but cooperation with it.

Take this example in the physical realm. Eating and drinking are not sufficient to make a person strong. They are important but not enough. Exercise is also necessary. So we in the spiritual realm must gladly choose, of our own free will, not only to know but to also do the will of God. Joshua said at one time in his life: "Choose you this day whom ye will serve" (Josh. 24:15). There is a choice that always has to be made when testing comes. The Holy Spirit is with us, but we must choose which way we are going. Joshua's choice was: "As for me and my house, we will serve the Lord" (v. 15).

When temptation comes, we must say no to the temptation and yes to the Lord. We are admonished in Romans 6 not to let sin reign in our bodies (v. 12). How can we do this except by turning ourselves over to the Holy Spirit? We must cooperate with Him by choosing.

It is a good thing to desire to be loving, but a definite effort to be loving is even better. None of this will work for us, however, unless God also works. The Scripture tells us that He works in us both to will and to do of His good pleasure. He creates the desire and also performs the work. But between the forming of the desire and the doing of the work we must choose for the work to be done.

One of the greatest sins among Christians today is the sin of indecision. According to James 4 the Holy Spirit yearns over us with a jealous love, for He wants God's will done in our lives.

In Galatians Paul said that the Spirit desires against the flesh and the flesh against the Spirit (5:17). This matter can be settled in each of our lives only as we choose which direction we will go. Though the fallen nature within us constantly wants us to sin, there is provision through the indwelling spirit for complete victory over those evil desires. The choice lies with us. This is why the apostle said in verse 16: "Walk in the Spirit, and ye shall not fulfil the lust of the flesh."

It is our yieldedness to the Spirit and dependence on Him that results in His defeating the evil nature. More than this, the Spirit of God also produces in the life of the believer what is pleasing to God.

Many of us have power steering or power brakes on our cars. These do not work automatically; they must be activated either by a movement of the hand on the steering wheel or of the foot on the brake pedal. In neither case is a great deal of strength needed on the part of the driver because of the power of these mechanical units in the automobile.

The analogy with regard to the work of the Spirit of God within us is clear. It is good to know that we are crucified with Christ and that we live, yet not us but Christ lives in us. It is glorious to know that the life which we now live in the flesh we live by the faith of the Son of God (Gal. 2:20). However, for this to be effective, we must trust

Him. We must turn our lives over to Him moment by moment. We make the choice, and He does the work.

Maintaining the Filling of the Spirit

Not only do we have the command in the fifth chapter of Ephesians to be filled with the Spirit (v. 18), but the next two verses also show how we are to maintain this fullness or control of the Spirit. The words are "Speaking to yourselves in psalms and hymns and spiritual songs, singing and making melody in your heart to the Lord; giving thanks always for all things unto God and the Father in the name of our Lord Jesus Christ" (vv. 19,20).

As additional help in this area, notice the words of Psalm 1:1-3: "Blessed is the man that walketh not in the counsel of the ungodly, nor standeth in the way of sinners, nor sitteth in the seat of the scornful. But his delight is in the law of the Lord; and in his law doth he meditate day and night. And he shall be like a tree planted by the rivers of water, that bringeth forth his fruit in his season; his leaf also shall not wither; and whatsoever he doeth shall prosper."

These two portions of Scripture suggest the devotional life that the Christian must maintain if the Spirit of God is to sustain control. Included is joyous thanksgiving, prayer and meditation in the Word. It calls for separation from ungodly companions and their wicked counsel. Spiritual prosperity will result as we delight ourselves in the Word and meditate on it. We will be like trees planted near running water that bring forth their fruit in season.

The spiritual truth is that when the Holy Spirit controls our lives, He produces the fruit of the Spirit, which spells prosperity for us in the life that pleases God.

God has made abundant provision for us through Christ so that we can live this life in the Spirit. Paul wrote to the Ephesians: "Blessed be the God and Father of our Lord Jesus Christ, who hath blessed us with all spiritual blessings in heavenly places in Christ" (1:3).

Peter stated the same truth in the following words, "According as his divine power hath given unto us all things that pertain unto life and godliness" (II Pet. 1:3). This is a most remarkable provision, but if we would benefit by it, we must dig into the Word of God regularly and meditate on it daily. In this way God will reveal to us sin in our lives, and this then can be confessed and our hearts cleansed. At the same time, He will produce righteousness in our lives because of our allowing the Holy Spirit absolute control.

The very presence of the Spirit is for the completion of God's work in us. This is what Ephesians 1:13 tells us: "In whom also after that ye believed, ye were sealed with that holy Spirit of promise, which is the earnest of our inheritance until the redemption of the purchased possession, unto the praise of his glory." God guarantees to finish what He has begun in our lives. This is clear also from Philippians 1:6: "Being confident of this very thing, that he which hath begun a good work in you will perform it until the day of Jesus Christ."

God has done His part; now He wants us to cooperate with Him, which is simply our turning over of our lives completely to the direction of the

Holy Spirit. This cooperation also includes our going to the Word to be built up through daily regular fellowship with the Lord through His Word.

Further light is thrown on this in John 6. Our Saviour said, "He that eateth my flesh, and drinketh my blood, dwelleth in me, and I in him. As the living Father hath sent me, and I live by the Father: so he that eateth me, even he shall live by me" (vv. 56,57). These are startling statements, and some have found them hard to understand, but the 63rd verse of the same chapter explains what the Saviour meant: "It is the spirit that quickeneth; the flesh profiteth nothing: the words that I speak unto you, they are spirit, and they are life." The Lord Jesus identifies Himself with the Word and communicates Himself through that Word. We must take the written Word into our lives and hearts and meditate on it, and the Holy Spirit will use it to produce the life of Christ in us.

So then, to sustain the filling of the Holy Spirit we must abide in Christ. The Lord Jesus said, "Abide in me, and I in you. As the branch cannot bear fruit of itself, except it abide in the vine; no more can ye, except ye abide in me" (John 15:4). We abide in Him by the Word, not by merely reading it but by meditating on it and making it part of ourselves in our thinking and praying. Just as we take food and assimilate it for physical strength, so we are to partake of the written Word in faith and under the direction of the Holy Spirit so that we might be spiritually strong.

When we are in communion with our Lord on this basis, we will realize the promise in the words: "Ye shall ask what ye will, and it shall be done unto you" (v. 7). Unless we maintain a daily fellowship with the Lord, we will fail and fall along the way.

The people of Israel were told to gather manna every day. It is the same for us in the spiritual realm. There must be a daily reading of the Word and submission to what it teaches us. Through the Word the Holy Spirit convicts us of sin and of righteousness. We will come to see things in our lives we did not realize were there, and God will not only show us what these things are but will also give us the grace and the power to overcome them. Let us not neglect this.

Results of Being Filled With the Spirit

A Spirit-controlled person will first of all realize and enjoy all the various ministries of the Spirit. The first of these is a regenerated life. Because of this new life we are no longer the persons we once were but are made new in Christ Jesus. This is a wonderful truth. Do we enjoy it? We will enjoy it if the Holy Spirit is controlling us according to God's pattern.

Another glorious result is that Christ indwells us. We are also in Him. Paul was certainly rejoicing when he wrote, "I am crucified with Christ: nevertheless I live; yet not I, but Christ liveth in me: and the life which I now live in the flesh I live by the faith of the Son of God, who loved me, and gave himself for me" (Gal. 2:20). I could not live this life on my own, but since I am the recipient of His life, this can be realized in me.

Another special ministry of the Spirit is that of anointing. Whatever the Lord calls us to do, He specially prepares us for it. This is another reason for rejoicing in the ministry of the Spirit.

His sanctifying work is also part of His ministry, as we have seen. By this, we mean that He has set us apart from certain things in our lives and set us apart totally unto God. He separates us from bad habits and produces in us habits of righteousness.

The Holy Spirit also produces a Christlike character in us. This character is described in Galatians 5:22,23—the fruit of the Spirit. It is not the fruit of human effort and moral and spiritual striving but the direct flow of the divine character from the Spirit through us, such as love, joy, peace and long-suffering.

In contrast to this, of course, is the work of the flesh. A translation that states the work of the flesh in language we are more used to says, "But when you follow your own wrong inclinations, your lives will produce these evil results: impure thoughts; eagerness for lustful pleasure, idolatry, spiritism . . . , hatred and fighting, jealousy and anger; constant effort to get the best for yourself, complaints and criticisms, . . . envy, murder, drunkenness, wild parties, and all that sort of thing. Let me tell you again as I have before, that anyone living that sort of life will not inherit the kingdom of God" (vv. 19-21). This is the work of the flesh. Just think of what the Holy Spirit saves us from! It is the natural tendency of our fleshly nature to pull us in this direction, even after we are saved; but when the Spirit comes in and takes control, He subdues these natural appetites and begins to produce the fruit of the Spirit in us.

101

If we walk after the Spirit, we will not fulfill the lust of the flesh, we are told in Galatians 5:16. And if we live in the Spirit, we should also walk in the Spirit. Since we have been saved through the operation of the Holy Spirit, let us not think that we can develop in the Christian life in the flesh. The Spirit of God is necessary for our Christian growth.

The result in Christian service will be according to I Corinthians 12:4-6: "Now God gives us many kinds of special abilities, but it is the same Holy Spirit who is the source of them all. There are different kinds of services to God, but it is the same Lord we are serving. There are many ways in which God works in our lives, but it is the same God who does the work in and through all of us who are His." The Holy Spirit displays God's power through each one of us as a means of helping the entire Church of God. The Holy Spirit works in us mightily in the service of the Lord, dividing to each one of us gifts as they are needed. He then exercises these gifts through us so that there will be no duplications. Just as in the physical body every member has its own task to do, so if we are under His control, He will give us power and grace and strength to do our work.

Chapter 7

Specific Gifts Mentioned

Before beginning this study of the spiritual gifts, read Chapters 12, 13 and 14 of I Corinthians carefully. That is the passage of Scripture dealt with here.

These three chapters set forth instructions concerning the gifts of the Holy Spirit. In Chapter 12 Paul wrote about the spiritual gifts given to believers; in Chapter 13 he told how these gifts are to be administered; in Chapter 14 he made specific corrections of the misuse of certain gifts.

In this chapter we will enumerate the gifts, explaining them in some detail, and learn how we may be filled with the Holy Spirit so that our lives may be used of God.

The gifts of the Holy Spirit are freely given to empower us to serve Christ. They are mentioned in I Corinthians 12, beginning with verse 8.

Words of Wisdom and Knowledge

The first gift mentioned is "the word of wisdom" (I Cor. 12:8). This is the power to speak with wisdom, to give the message with discretion and spiritual understanding. Then there is "the word of knowledge," another gift given to some people (v. 8). This is the power to speak with practical intelligence, to make the message understandable.

Words of wisdom deal with the deep things of God, whereas words of knowledge help make clear and intelligible the deep things of God.

The Gift of Faith

Listed in I Corinthians 12:9 is the gift of faith. This is not the faith necessary for salvation. That, too, is a gift, for we read in Ephesians 2:8: "For by grace are ye saved through faith; and that not of yourselves: it is the gift of God." But the gift of faith mentioned in I Corinthians 12 refers to faith by which great exploits for God may be accomplished.

This kind of faith has been illustrated by such men as Moses, who was able, by faith, to bring about great miracles in Egypt, at the Red Sea and in the desert. It was illustrated by Joshua at the Jordan River and at the city of Jericho.

It was also illustrated by David when he overcame Goliath by his faith in God. It was illustrated by Gideon, who drove out great armies with 300 men. Peter demonstrated this kind of faith when he walked out on the sea toward Jesus. Paul evidenced it in his Christian walk. It was illustrated by such men as Hudson Taylor, who did missionary work in China by faith, and George Mueller, who was able, by faith in God, to do great things for a large number of orphans in England. Even today certain believers are accomplishing great things for God because they are willing to believe Him. Faith is a wonderful gift of the Holy Spirit.

Gifts of Healing and Miracles

Next, Paul mentioned the "gifts of healing" (I Cor. 12:9). This is power to cure diseases. But please note that it may be by means of medication, surgery or prayer and faith. We cannot limit it to one of these. It is the ability to restore health, and the method is not the important question.

Another gift, mentioned in verse 10, is "the working of miracles," a supernatural power given to some to do great deeds or to work wonders beyond the power of ordinary men.

The Gift of Prophecy

Next is the gift of prophecy, which is really the gift of preaching, or forthtelling, as well as foretelling. Some people have a special ability to see things as they are happening and to understand how they harmonize with Scripture. This is prophetic insight. Speaking to edify, exhort and comfort people is preaching. Some people are great orators, but they may not necessarily have the gift of prophecy at all. One who is a prophet speaks so that people are moved to action because of the power of the Spirit of God in his message.

Discerning of Spirits

Another gift of the Spirit is that of "discerning of spirits" (I Cor. 12:10), which means the power to distinguish between the works of the Holy Spirit and those of false, or evil, spirits.

This gift was very necessary when Paul was writing because the Word of God was then being

105

given. Men of God were writing by inspiration, but other writing was being done that was not inspired by God and was not to be part of God's Word. Someone had to have the gift of discerning which was inspired and which was not. Thank God for that gift!

It is still necessary today because of the many false cults and doctrines that are springing up everywhere. We need people who are able to discern whether or not something is from God. Of course, the Spirit will enlighten us through His Word, and we need the ability to discern spiritual matters, to distinguish between imitation gifts and those that are genuine. Satan often comes as an angel of light, and he may imitate some of the gifts.

This gift of discernment is lacking in many churches today. The fact that a preacher names the name of Jesus Christ does not mean that he is a gospel preacher. He may be able to leave out the gospel altogether and fool many people. We need to discern whether or not men are preaching the Word of God.

Gifts of Tongues and Interpreting

Another of the gifts mentioned in I Corinthians 12 is the gift of "divers kinds of tongues" (v. 10). This means a variety of tongues, or languages. Along with this gift, Paul listed "the interpretation of tongues" (v. 10), or explaining what was said in another language.

These gifts, as well as all the others listed, were distributed to each individual as God willed. Some people think all believers must speak in tongues,

106

but God says that the gift is given to whom the Spirit desires.

Proper Order of the Gifts

Note that after God has given gifts to Christians, He gives these gifted believers to the Church: "And God hath set some in the church, first apostles, secondarily prophets, thirdly teachers, after that miracles, then gifts of healings, helps, governments, diversities of tongues" (I Cor. 12:28).

Ephesians 4:11-13 also mentions that these gifted believers are given to the Church: "And he gave some, apostles; and some, prophets; and some, evangelists; and some, pastors and teachers; for the perfecting of the saints, for the work of the ministry, for the edifying of the body of Christ: till we all come in the unity of the faith."

Notice the order in which these gifted believers are listed in I Corinthians 12:28: "First apostles." This word "apostles" refers to those chosen by God to be His special messengers. It was their responsibility to lay the foundation of the Church.

Second, He has given some prophets. The gift of prophecy referred to preachers, those who expounded God's Word to edify, exhort and comfort others.

Paul next mentioned teachers. They are believers who have the ability to explain God's Word in a way that promotes spiritual growth.

Listed next is miracles. This gift involves the use of supernatural powers to do great deeds, to work wonders, to accomplish great things that only

God can do through gifted believers. These miracles may be physical ones, or they may be miracles of grace (of a spiritual nature).

After that is listed healings. As already mentioned, this involves the power to cure diseases, whether by medicine, surgery or prayer and faith.

Helps, listed next in I Corinthians 12:28, has to do with people who have aptness to support, undergird or uphold others. Governments is the gift of those who can manage, organize or guide others.

Finally, Paul mentioned "diversities of tongues." As already mentioned, this gift involved the ability to speak in a variety of languages for the edification of others.

Let us remember the order of importance of these gifts as God has given them.

Verses 29 and 30 say, "Are all apostles? Are all prophets? Are all teachers? Are all workers of miracles? Have all the gifts of healing? Do all speak with tongues? Do all interpret?" The obvious answer to all these questions is no. The Holy Spirit knows how to distribute the gifts wisely. Not every believer will have the same gift, and no one believer will have all the gifts. Let us trust the Word of God and not demand gifts which He has not offered us. He gives the gifts as He wills.

Chapter 8

Genuine Gifts or Imitations

After discussing the spiritual gifts and before correcting the misuse of some of these gifts, Paul discussed a matter in I Corinthians 13 which can be used as a basis for determining whether special gifts are from the Holy Spirit or from another source.

Source of Gifts

Can anyone else give gifts similar to those listed in I Corinthians 12? Yes, definitely! The Scriptures make it very clear that Satan often comes as an angel of light (II Cor. 11:14) and imitates some of the gifts of the Holy Spirit.

It is important that we know the difference between the gifts of the Holy Spirit and the imitations of those gifts. You can determine whether the gift that you possess (or claim to possess) is a gift of the Holy Spirit or an imitation by Satan through the test found in Chapter 13 of I Corinthians.

All gifts given to believers by the Holy Spirit are to be profitable, but when the gifts are only imitations and when they are not properly administered through love, they lead to pride, conceit and slander. Often those who do not possess the gifts of the Holy Spirit or who do not use them in love speak evil of, and make false accusations against,

109

those who do not agree with them. Such people are useless to God. These are piercing statements, but they are based on the truths found in I Corinthians 13.

Misuse of Gifts

The first gift which Paul mentioned in Chapter 13 was misused in the Corinthian church and, unfortunately, is also misused today. This was the gift of tongues. "Though I speak with the tongues [languages] of men and of angels, and have not charity [love], I am become as sounding brass, or a tinkling cymbal" (v. 1). In other words, if I had the gift of speaking in languages—not only the thousands of languages of men but also the languages of the angels—but did not use that gift in love, I would be as sounding brass or a tinkling cymbal. I would just be making a noise.

Some people use all their energy just to blow their whistles and have none left for accomplishing anything constructive. In the same way some people misuse the gifts that God has given them (if what they have is really genuine and not an imitation).

Paul also mentioned other gifts: "And though I have the gift of prophecy, and understand all mysteries, and all knowledge; and though I have all faith, so that I could remove mountains, and have not charity [love], I am nothing. And though I bestow all my goods to feed the poor, and though I give my body to be burned, and have not charity [love], it profiteth me nothing" (vv. 2,3).

The Greek language has three words for love.

110

One refers to sensual love. Another is used to express filial love, parental love or brotherly love, a love based on emotions. The third word is used for the highest kind of love—a constant, unselfish love from the will which reaches out to others regardless of their worthiness or response. This last one is the word used in I Corinthians 13. It is not found in secular Greek literature, for it is not a secular word. It is not a love that can be demonstrated in the lives of unsaved people. "God so loved the world" (John 3:16). He is love.

When a person is born again, the Spirit of God takes His place in that person's life and sheds abroad His love in that heart (Rom. 5:5). If you and I are truly born again, we possess the Holy Spirit. And if we possess Him, this love, which is a fruit of the Spirit, is shed abroad in our hearts.

The gifts which we receive from the Holy Spirit are the manifestations of the Spirit's presence within our lives. But if we are to show that they are genuine gifts of the Holy Spirit, they must be accompanied by the love and other qualities of the fruit of the Spirit, which God puts into our hearts. If that fruit is consistently missing from your life, it is a sign that the Holy Spirit has not yet entered your heart; you are not yet born again. "If any man have not the Spirit of Christ, he is none of his" (Rom. 8:9).

Imitation of Gifts

Therefore, it is necessary for us to test the spirits, according to the Scriptures (I John 4:1). That does not mean that we should test the Holy

111

Spirit. We should test the gifts which we believe are from the Spirit to see if they are accompanied by love. If they are, we have proof that the Holy Spirit is within our lives and is the author of these gifts. If they are not accompanied and administered by love, it is possible that the gifts which we claim to possess are imitations produced by Satan.

Does Satan ever imitate the work of the Holy Spirit? Moses threw down his rod before Pharaoh, and it became a serpent. Pharaoh's wise men and sorcerers, who were the workers of Satan, threw down their rods, and they became serpents too (see Ex. 7:10-13). The sorcerers also imitated several of the plagues brought upon Egypt. Satan can and does imitate some of the works of the Holy Spirit. Anything of a supernatural nature must be tested to see whether it is from God or from Satan, for Satan is seeking to deceive as many as he can (Matt. 24:24; I Tim. 4:1). Many people have been enchanted by the supernatural power evident in spiritism and occultism, but the Scriptures emphatically forbid these practices because the power is from Satan (see Deut. 18:10-12). Satan can imitate the gifts of the Holy Spirit; he often imitates the gift of prophecy (see Acts 16:16-18). Satan can deceive in very subtle ways (see Mark 8:31-33; Acts 5:1-5). Satan constantly imitates the power and work of the Holy Spirit.

Some things, however, Satan cannot imitate. He cannot imitate the grace of God, the graces of the Holy Spirit or God's love. He cannot imitate those things which are mentioned in Galatians 5:22,23—love, joy, peace, long-suffering, gentleness, goodness, faith, meekness and temperance—because they are the fruit of the Spirit.

112

Some of the so-called proofs of the filling of the Holy Spirit are not proofs at all because they are not administered in love. Therefore, they prove that they are not the gifts of the Holy Spirit but are imitations. The manifestation of God's love is the real proof of one's being filled with the Holy Spirit and gifted by Him, for the gifts of the Holy Spirit must be administered in love.

Satan has caused some people to say that we at the Back to the Bible Broadcast do not believe in the gifts of the Holy Spirit. That is not true. We are not arguing against the gifts; we are trying to correct the false use of them. We have also been accused of attributing to Satan some of the work of the Holy Spirit. Nothing is further from the truth. We are trying to show that some things which people call the works of the Holy Spirit are actually imitations produced by Satan.

We must conclude that what we often call the gifts of the Holy Spirit are imitations unless they are accompanied by love and by the other graces of the Holy Spirit, which are mentioned in Galatians 5:22,23. That is why Paul said, "Though I speak with the tongues of men [which Satan can imitate] and of angels [which Satan, having been an angel, can also imitate], and have not charity, I am become as sounding brass, or a tinkling cymbal. And though I have the gift of prophecy, and understand all mysteries, and all knowledge; and though I have all faith, so that I could remove mountains, and have not charity, I am nothing" (I Cor. 13:1,2).

Tongues, or languages, which are not used with a God-given love are as unintelligible as clanging brass and tinkling cymbals. Suppose that I have faith to perform great and marvelous wonders—

113

even to remove mountains. If that faith is not per-
meated with love, it means absolutely nothing. If
the works that I do are not controlled by love,
they are worthless.

Chapter 9

The Gift of Tongues

As we study the Book of I Corinthians, we learn that the church of Corinth possessed all of the spiritual gifts (see I Cor. 1:5-7). But there were divisions in the church of Corinth (see vv. 10,11). Pride had become evident, and many of the people were still babes in Christ (see 3:1-3). And so they were admonished to love and to seek the best gifts, one of which is prophecy (see 12:31; 14:1). They were not to be content merely with the things that belong to babes in Christ.

The gift of tongues, or languages, edified the person speaking (v. 4), but whenever an interpreter was not present, they were to be quiet (v. 28). Paul said that he had spoken in tongues, or languages, many times (v. 18). This was one of the gifts given when the Spirit came.

When the Spirit enters the life, that is the beginning, not the consummation, of that life. Some believe that once they have received the Spirit and spoken in tongues they have reached the zenith. But God says that receiving the Spirit at salvation is the beginning; from there we are to continue.

In the chapters under discussion, Paul was trying to correct the misuse of gifts. Before the misuse of something can be corrected, it is necessary to understand its proper use.

Some people say that I do not believe in

115

tongues. I may startle you by saying that I do believe in tongues if and when the gift is used in the proper way and at the proper time. This statement may be misquoted by some who insist that the present "tongues" movement is inspired by the Devil. I do not wish to be misunderstood; therefore, I ask that you give careful attention to this problem so that you will know what God has to say. I have spent much time studying this subject. I have also read a great deal of literature on the subject and have analyzed it to see whether or not it agrees with Scripture.

Prophecy Concerning the Holy Spirit

Before discussing the proper use of tongues, I would like to consider several passages of Scripture. The first is Acts 2:16-18, which contains a quotation from the prophecy of Joel: "But this is that which was spoken by the prophet Joel; And it shall come to pass in the last days, saith God, I will pour out of my Spirit upon all flesh: and your sons and your daughters shall prophesy, and your young men shall see visions, and your old men shall dream dreams: and on my servants and on my handmaidens I will pour out in those days of my Spirit; and they shall prophesy."

Twice in those verses it is said that the Spirit will be poured out upon all flesh, after which men and women will prophesy. Visions and dreams are mentioned but not tongues.

John the Baptist said, "But he that cometh after me ... shall baptize you with the Holy Ghost, and with fire" (Matt. 3:11). Compare this verse with the words of Jesus in Acts 1:5: "For

116

John truly baptized with water; but ye shall be baptized with the Holy Ghost not many days hence."

Why did Jesus not say exactly what John said? John said, "Shall baptize you with the Holy Ghost, and with fire." Jesus did not include the words "and with fire" because He was referring only to the coming of the Spirit at Pentecost. The prophecy of John the Baptist was only partially fulfilled at that time. The complete fulfillment will come either in the fire of judgment at the Second Coming of Christ or shortly before that time, during the Tribulation.

Prophecy Fulfilled

Acts 2:4 records the fulfillment of the first part of this prophecy. The disciples were baptized by the Holy Spirit, and they were also filled with Him. The ministry of the Holy Spirit is to indwell the believer and to fill him for service. The latter part of the prophecy of John the Baptist awaits fulfillment.

Let us study some of these words in the original language. God gave us the New Testament in the Greek language, which is very expressive, especially in the use of verb tenses. Translators have done their best to give us the meaning of the verb tenses, but in many cases this cannot be done in a word or two.

The Greek word for "filled" is in the aorist tense in Acts 2:4, which indicates that the action happened at a point of time in the past. When the Holy Spirit came at Pentecost, He baptized the Church into the Body of Christ (see I Cor. 12:13).

117

Then He empowered the believers for service. They were filled with the Holy Spirit so that they might witness. Today each believer is baptized into the Body of Christ at that point in time when he is saved; he is also filled, or controlled, by the Spirit at that time. But the control of the Spirit can be hindered by sin. This is why we are commanded to be filled with the Spirit (Eph. 5:18). The filling will be a repeated action as we recognize and confess sin in our lives.

Other Languages

At Pentecost the disciples "began to speak with other tongues, as the Spirit gave them utterance" (Acts 2:4). In other words, the Holy Spirit gave them the ability to speak in languages that they had never learned. Jewish people from many different countries were gathered together in Jerusalem during Pentecost. The languages of those countries were foreign to the disciples, who were Galileans. Yet, when they were filled with the Spirit, they spoke in words that were understood by the visitors from those foreign lands.

The word "tongues" in Acts 2:4 is the translation of the Greek word *glossa*, which primarily refers to the physical organ of our body which we call the tongue. A secondary meaning is "language." The context of any passage in which this word occurs will show which meaning it should be given. For example, if someone says, "I burned my tongue," he is referring to the organ in his mouth. But when a person says, "I speak the native tongue," he is referring to a spoken language.

In Acts 2:4 the words "speak with other

118

tongues" mean that the disciples spoke in languages different from their own. In Acts 2:6,8 a different Greek word is used: *dialektos.* Our English word "dialect" is derived from this word. This Greek word always refers to languages; it has no other meaning. These verses show that the disciples were divinely enabled to speak not only the different languages spoken by the visitors but also the different dialects of the same languages. The Phrygians and Pamphylians both spoke Greek but in different dialects. Even the dialect of Judea differed from that of Galilee (see Mark 14:70; Acts 2:7-11).

So the gift of tongues was the divine enablement to speak in a language not previously learned by the one speaking it. The languages spoken were understood by those who heard them.

Speaking Boldly

There is a significant truth in Acts 4:31: "And when they had prayed, the place was shaken where they were assembled together; and they were all filled with the Holy Ghost, and they spake the word of God with boldness."

In addition to the disciples, other people were gathered together. They were no doubt new Christians, and they were filled with the Holy Spirit. They began to speak, but it was not in other tongues. They spoke "the word of God with boldness." The literal translation of this is "They began to prophesy." This is another of the gifts of the Holy Spirit.

In both cases (Acts 2 and 4) the people were

119

filled, and yet they spoke in different ways. In the one case they spoke another language; in the other case they prophesied, or spoke, the Word of God.

First Corinthians 14:1-3 mentions both of these gifts: "Follow after charity [love], and desire spiritual gifts, but rather that ye may prophesy. For he that speaketh in an unknown tongue speaketh not unto men, but unto God: ... howbeit in the spirit he speaketh mysteries. But he that prophesieth speaketh unto men to edification, and exhortation, and comfort." (Note that the word "unknown" in verse 2 was not in the original but was added by the translators.)

In Acts 13:9-11 it is recorded that Paul, filled with the Holy Spirit, spoke with authority. But in this case he did not speak in tongues or prophesy. He spoke words of judgment to a tool of Satan who called himself Bar-jesus (son of Jesus), or Elymas. Paul pronounced judgment on this evil man, but he had to be filled with the Spirit before he could do so.

Acts 19:6 mentions both tongues and prophecy as evidences of the Spirit's presence: "And when Paul had laid his hands upon them, the Holy Ghost came on them; and they spake with tongues, and prophesied."

We see from these passages that there is no ground for concluding that the initial sign of a person's receiving the Holy Spirit, or being baptized by the Holy Spirit, was the ability to speak in tongues. The coming of the Holy Spirit on men and women was manifested in a number of different ways. And the gift of tongues does not hold a prominent place. The gift of prophecy far outweighs it, as do other spiritual gifts.

We also see from these passages that the gifts were used to exalt Jesus Christ. Particularly on the Day of Pentecost, we note that when Peter spoke, tongues fell into the background and Jesus Christ came to the foreground. Christ declared before the Spirit came that, when He did come, He would glorify Christ (John 16:13-15). This is demonstrated throughout the Book of the Acts. It is not men, it is not gifts, it is not even the Spirit of God Himself who is prominent, but the Person of the Lord Jesus Christ is exalted above all. This should be the test of every believer's life and ministry. What are we exalting? Is it self, the gift or the Saviour?

Chapter 10

The Use and Abuse of Tongues

At least 16 spiritual gifts were given to the various members of the early church. They are listed in such passages as Romans 12:3-8; I Corinthians 12—14 and Ephesians 4:7-16. Some of these gifts are given to believers today; others, such as the gift of apostleship, are not.

Gifts of the Spirit are not to be confused with the natural abilities of God's people. Undoubtedly, these natural abilities are sanctified and enriched by the Holy Spirit, making them of service to the Lord. But spiritual gifts are related to the new birth, while natural abilities are related to physical birth. The gifts named in the preceding Bible passages have their source in God (see Rom. 12:3), are provided through Christ as the result of His triumphant resurrection and ascension (see Eph. 4:7-16), and are distributed by the sovereign will of the Holy Spirit (see I Cor. 12:8-11).

In the church at Corinth a great deal of interest and also confusion centered in the gift of tongues. Apparently, something about this gift caught the attention of the Corinthian believers, many of whom had been delivered from a life of corruption through the missionary work of the Apostle Paul. The priority they gave this gift caused the apostle, under the inspiration of the Holy Spirit, to deal with certain miracle gifts of the Spirit. He showed what place the tongues gift had in relation to them and corrected the abuses that had developed in Corinth concerning it.

In view of the continuing interest today in speaking in tongues, we will do well to consider what the New Testament has to say concerning it. Experience is not our guide. In order to know what is right concerning a subject of this nature, we must learn what the Bible says about it and guide our experience by the Word. We must never let experience take the place of God's revelation.

Two books in the New Testament furnish the background for a study of this subject. One is the Book of the Acts, a book of history, and the other is I Corinthians, a book of doctrine and moral instruction.

In the Book of the Acts, three chapters contain specific information about the gift of tongues. Chapter 2, dealing with the coming of the Holy Spirit at Pentecost, describes the initial appearance of the gift.

We read in Acts 10 that the Holy Spirit came on new Gentile believers and they spoke in tongues. We know from Peter's words that the gift of tongues evidenced in the household of Cornelius was the same as that given on the Day of Pentecost. As he related the event to the Jewish Christians in Jerusalem, Peter said, "As I began to speak, the Holy Ghost fell on them, as on us at the beginning" (Acts 11:15).

In Acts 19 certain disciples of John were brought up to date by Paul on what God had done through the Lord Jesus and through the Holy Spirit. When Paul laid his hands on these new believers in Christ, the Holy Spirit came on them "and they spake with tongues, and prophesied" (v. 6).

Tongues at Pentecost

The nature of the gift of tongues as revealed in Acts 2 has been dealt with in Chapter 9. The gift of tongues at Pentecost was the Spirit-given ability to tell of "the wonderful works of God" (Acts 2:11) in a language not previously known by the one speaking it. No interpreters were needed at Pentecost because the languages spoken were understood by those who heard them.

Purpose of Tongues

One purpose of this remarkable gift was to gain the attention of the multitude which came together and heard Peter's stirring message concerning the Lord Jesus Christ. Another, and a more important, purpose was to provide a sign to the Jews, through this miracle gift, that God was doing a special work among them.

The Law was given under remarkable demonstrations of power at Sinai. So it is to be expected that the beginning of God's new work at Pentecost would also involve supernatural manifestations. Concerning the latter, the writer to the Hebrews stated, "How shall we escape, if we neglect so great salvation; which at the first began to be spoken by the Lord, and was confirmed unto us by them that heard him; God also bearing them witness, both with signs and wonders, and with divers miracles, and gifts of the Holy Ghost, according to his own will?" (Heb. 2:3,4).

The miracles done by our Lord were evidence, or credentials, proving Him to be the Messiah. When John the Baptist wondered if the Lord Jesus was actually the Messiah, our Saviour's answer was, "Go and shew John again those things which ye do hear and see: the blind receive their sight, and the lame walk, the lepers are cleansed, and the deaf hear, the dead are raised up, and the poor have the gospel preached to them" (Matt. 11:4,5).

This message was clear to many of the Jewish people. They understood the significance of the miracles and works of Christ better than their leaders did and said, "When the Christ shall come, He will not perform more signs than those which this man has, will He?" (John 7:31, NASB).

Paul's ministry and message were also confirmed through remarkable gifts. He wrote to the Romans: "For I will not dare to speak of any of those things which Christ hath not wrought by me, to make the Gentiles obedient, by word and deed, through mighty signs and wonders, by the power of the Spirit of God; so that from Jerusalem, and round about unto Illyricum, I have fully preached the gospel of Christ" (Rom. 15:18,19).

It was a characteristic of the Jews to look for signs (see Matt. 16:4; John 4:48; I Cor. 1:22). It was also, as we have seen, God's plan to confirm, by special signs, the gospel message and its messengers wherever He deemed it necessary. Every great forward step of the gospel recorded in the Book of the Acts was characterized by certain signs. At Pentecost the noise like a rushing, violent wind, the tongues as of fire and the speaking in foreign languages were God's stamp of approval both on the

125

messengers and on the message. The audience was primarily Jewish, so the sign-gifts were in keeping with His purpose.

When Peter went to the house of Cornelius, he took six Jewish men with him (Acts 10:23,24; 11:12). The gospel was taking a new step forward; Gentiles were going to turn to the Lord. The evidence of God's working in their hearts was confirmed by their speaking in tongues. This convinced Peter and the six Jewish brethren with him. It also silenced the criticism of the Jewish Christians in Jerusalem when they criticized Peter for going to the house of Cornelius (see 11:15-18).

Peter referred to this matter again at the council in Jerusalem. There he emphasized the fact that God had chosen him to present the gospel to the Gentiles and had confirmed His divine working in the Gentile hearts by giving them the Holy Spirit (15:7,8).

The disciples of John the Baptist who came to a saving knowledge of Christ through Paul's ministry in Ephesus spoke in tongues and prophesied when the Holy Spirit came on them (19:1-7). This manifestation of the Spirit's power constituted a sign to those men of Jewish background that Paul's message was from God.

It is one thing for God to offer signs to prove the truth of His message; it is something else when a Christian seeks for signs before he will believe God. One who does this is a babe in Christ rather than a mature believer. Seeking for a sign, whether it is the gift of tongues or something else, indicates that the person has a weak faith rather than a strong faith.

126

An example of this is found in John 20:24,25: "But Thomas, one of the twelve, called Didymus, was not with them when Jesus came. The other disciples therefore said unto him, We have seen the Lord. But he said unto them, Except I shall see in his hands the print of the nails, and put my finger into the print of the nails, and thrust my hand into his side, I will not believe." This man, who was weak in faith, demanded to see before he would believe. He was just like many of the Corinthians, who apparently thought they needed the gift of tongues as evidence of their being filled with the Holy Spirit.

Notice what Jesus did about Thomas's unbelief: "And after eight days again his disciples were within, and Thomas with them: then came Jesus, the doors being shut, and stood in the midst, and said, Peace be unto you. Then saith he to Thomas, Reach hither thy finger, and behold my hands; and reach hither thy hand, and thrust it into my side: and be not faithless, but believing" (vv. 26,27).

Our Lord gave Thomas this evidence so that he would have faith. At the same time Jesus said, "Thomas, because thou hast seen me, thou hast believed: blessed are they that have not seen, and yet have believed" (v. 29).

In I Corinthians 1:22 Paul said, "For the Jews require a sign." Some will not believe unless they can see.

Romans 4:20-22 says that although Abraham could not see the fulfillment of the promise, he believed God and, therefore, God counted it to him for righteousness. Abraham was strong in faith and did not require a sign.

The unbelieving Jews wanted a sign, but Jesus said, "An evil and adulterous generation seeketh after a sign; and there shall no sign be given to it, but the sign of the prophet Jonas" (Matt. 12:39). A judicial sign is spoken of in I Corinthians 14:21, but that will be considered later.

Christ promised that the Holy Spirit would come to dwell within each believer (see John 14:16). Concerning the Spirit our Lord said, "If any man thirst let him come unto me, and drink. He that believeth on me, as the scripture hath said, out of his belly shall flow rivers of living water" (7:37,38).

God fills us with His Holy Spirit when we confess any sin in our lives and believe the promise concerning the Holy Spirit. We need no signs to know that we are filled. His Word tells us that if we confess our sins, allowing Him to control our lives, we are filled.

Often those who seek for a sign to assure themselves that they are filled with the Holy Spirit withdraw from the fellowship of other Christians who believe God's promise concerning the filling of the Spirit without a sign. Such sign-seeking Christians are usually very critical. They lack love in their hearts, which is part of the fruit of the Spirit. Their very attitude indicates that they are not filled with the Holy Spirit. Faith does not require sight (see Heb. 11).

In the accounts of speaking in tongues recorded in the Book of the Acts, not one person involved asked for the gift. It was bestowed by the Holy Spirit without their asking for it.

128

Not All Spoke in Tongues

Note also that speaking in tongues was not mentioned concerning the 3000 who received the Lord Jesus when Peter preached at Pentecost. Yet they had the assurance of receiving the Holy Spirit (see Acts 2:38). Miracles were not absent, but they were of another nature—of a moral and spiritual kind.

This multitude accepted as leaders men who had no standing as scholars or as religious leaders among the Jews. They accepted the simple ordinances of baptism and the Lord's Supper in place of the elaborate ritual of the temple.

The Jews believed, on the basis of Old Testament promises, that economic prosperity was the evidence of God's blessing. But these new converts gave up some of their wealth, sharing it with the less fortunate among them. They put their money into a common fund so that fellow believers would not suffer undue hardship.

Above all, this group had received as their Redeemer the One whom the leaders of their nation had rejected and had crucified through envy.

A similar pattern followed wherever the gospel message was preached, according to the record in Acts. The changing of people's minds—their new viewpoints and values and their devotion to the Person and work of Christ—finally led their opponents in Thessalonica to say that the Christians had turned the world upside down (see Acts 17:6). This was the evidence of the presence of the Holy Spirit and of His working in their hearts. Speaking in tongues is mentioned in Acts only in the three instances already discussed.

129

Tongues in Corinth

The Corinthian church had severe internal problems. It was undoubtedly the most carnal church to which Paul wrote (see I Cor. 3:1). And yet, they were enriched by Christ "in all utterance, and in all knowledge" (1:5). Paul covered the subject of knowledge in the early chapters of I Corinthians and the subject of speech, or utterance, in Chapters 12—14. These Corinthian believers were in no way inferior to other local church groups with regard to the special gifts of the Spirit (see 1:7). Nevertheless, with all these advantages, enough individuals in that church misused their privileges to characterize the whole group as "babes in Christ" (3:1).

It is evident from reading I Corinthians 12—14 that the tongues gift was given a very high place in the thinking of many of the Corinthian believers. That the inspired apostle did not share this view is also clear from the same passage.

Apparently the Corinthian believers regarded the gift of tongues as the best of the miracle gifts and considered those exercising it to be a sort of spiritual aristocracy. This gift was so abused among them that they were in danger of repulsing other believers, as well as unbelievers, who came into the church services (see I Cor. 14:23).

Nature of Tongues Gift at Corinth

Some Bible expositors think there is a marked difference between the gift of tongues referred to in Acts and the one discussed in I Corinthians. The position held by many is that the gift spoken of in the Book of the Acts was the ability to speak foreign languages without having learned them. They believe the gift referred to in I Corinthians was that of ecstatic utterances. Some translators have even used that expression in I Corinthians wherever the gift of tongues is mentioned. Others believe that ecstatic utterances characterized the gift from the beginning, even in the Book of the Acts. This idea, of course, will not stand up under examination.

Others, and we are among them, believe that the gift of tongues is the same in Acts as in I Corinthians.

The word "unknown," which is used as an adjective to qualify the word "tongue" or "tongues" in I Corinthians 14:4, is not in the original. This is made clear in the King James Version, where the word "unknown" is in italics. Furthermore, there is no good reason for the word "unknown" to have been added.

The words used in I Corinthians to describe this gift are the same as those used in the Book of the Acts. Compare such passages as Acts 10:46 and 19:6 with I Corinthians 14:5. The terminology in these passages is identical. And nothing in the context of I Corinthians suggests that anything other than languages were being referred to. Verse 1 of Chapter 13 is sometimes used as a proof that ecstatic utterances were meant, but as one of the great Greek expositors of a past generation stated, "The 'tongues of men' must mean the tongues spoken by men in general if language is to have its natural sense." The same would hold true for the tongues, or languages, of angels.

The word "tongue" appears eight times in I Corinthians 14. With one exception (v. 9), this

131

singular form of the word refers to the gift of tongues. In verse 9 the physical organ itself is meant. Paul said, "So likewise ye, except ye utter by the tongue words easy to be understood, how shall it be known what is spoken? For ye shall speak into the air" (v. 9). The plural form appears eight times also. Seven of the occurrences have to do with the gift of tongues. In verse 21, where the word "tongues" does not refer to the gift of tongues, it does have to do with foreign languages.

How can this changing from the singular to the plural with reference to this gift of the Holy Spirit be explained if it means ecstatic utterances? There is no problem if we recognize that the gift of tongues is the God-given ability to speak in a foreign language not previously known to the one speaking it. Furthermore, the manifestation of this gift is "words." These are not jumbled words or gibberish but words "easy to be understood" (v. 9).

Consider the word "barbarian" in verse 11. This has no reference to a person's religion but simply refers to his language. The ancient Egyptians considered anyone who could not speak Egyptian to be a foreigner. The Greeks picked up this racial snobbery and called anyone who could not speak Greek a "barbarian" or, in our language, a foreigner. So Paul said in verse 11 that if someone were to speak to him in a language which he could not understand, each would be a barbarian, or foreigner, to the other.

On the basis of this fact, Dr. Robert L. Thomas of Talbot Theological Seminary said in the May, 1963, issue of the *King's Business:* "If this verse referred to a man's incoherent, inarticulate sounds

132

which no living person could understand, it would not make him a foreigner but a babbler. The contrary would be true, however, if he spoke a foreign language."

In light of these facts, it seems more reasonable to understand the gift of tongues in Corinth to be the same as that given at Pentecost—the ability to speak in a foreign language not previously learned by the speaker.

Limitations of the Gift

The gift of tongues is definitely limited in its ministry. This is clear from the contrast which Paul drew between the gift of prophecy and the gift of tongues. He encouraged believers to seek spiritual gifts but to prefer the gift of prophecy over that of tongues (see I Cor. 14:1). One element of prophecy is that of telling forth the Word of God (see v. 3). This was closely related to what we call Bible teaching. Another element was the power to predict events and conditions (see Acts 11:27,28). A third element, essential at that time when the New Testament was not yet fully given, was the power to receive new truth from God (see I Cor. 14:30).

A gift of this nature was necessary to help God's people grow in grace and in the knowledge of our Lord Jesus Christ. In contrast to this, the tongues gift limited a man to some special experience with God that provided no service to the church unless he or someone else could interpret what was said.

This is why the Holy Spirit, through Paul, said that the man who had the prophetic gift was greater than the one who spoke in a foreign

133

tongue. The source of each gift was the same—the Holy Spirit. The service, however, was not the same. The gift of prophecy far exceeded the gift of tongues in this regard.

Because some might have placed a higher value on the personal benefits of speaking in a foreign tongue, the apostle went on to declare that even in the realm of communion and prayer the gift was limited. The man who prayed in a foreign tongue prayed in the Spirit, but his mind, his understanding, was not helped. He could not express to himself what he had felt in the experience of prayer, much less pass it on to others. Paul did not favor such an experience, for he said, "I will pray with the spirit, and I will pray with the understanding also" (I Cor. 14:15).

The gift of tongues was limited in its distribution; it was not available to all believers. "Do all speak with tongues?" the apostle asked (12:30). The answer is obvious. They do not! The gifts were distributed to the believers according to the will of the Spirit of God. None of the miracle gifts were common to all believers. Most certainly the gift of tongues was not given to each believer in the Corinthian church or in any other New Testament church. If the list in I Corinthians 12 is a standard for the importance of the various gifts, the gift of tongues was not first but last (see v. 28).

This does not support the teaching that the initial sign, or evidence, of the Holy Spirit's presence in a life is the gift of tongues. And regardless of whether one believes the gift of tongues to be foreign languages or ecstatic utterances, the limitation of its distribution still holds. Not all received it. The baptism of the Holy Spirit was for all believers, and according to I Corinthians 12:13 this was realized. But not every believer spoke in tongues. These two things should not be confused, because they are not the same. The baptism of the Spirit inducts believers into the Body of Christ, and every believer is a member of that Body. Few of them, however, have ever spoken in tongues.

The distribution of the miracle gifts was directed by the Holy Spirit (see vv. 7-11). To teach that all believers will speak in tongues, or should speak in tongues, contradicts this very clear passage. Nowhere in the Scriptures are believers told specifically to seek the gift of tongues. They are admonished to seek spiritual gifts but rather that they might prophesy (14:1). Thus, the gift of tongues is played down in this inspired admonition.

Rules Governing the Gift of Tongues

Chapter 14 of I Corinthians, which is the longest of this book's three chapters on spiritual gifts, deals with the limitations of a gift, rules covering its use and severe warnings concerning its abuse. No earnest believer who wants to please the Lord can treat this matter lightly. Neither should he draw from this chapter conclusions contrary to its whole meaning.

General Rules

Two general rules govern the use of tongues. We have already touched on the first one. It concerns the fact that the Apostle Paul encouraged the Corinthians to seek spiritual gifts but stated a preference for prophecy rather than for tongues. Anyone who claims to be directed by the Spirit of God but who changes the divine order and emphasis in relation to these two gifts is going contrary to the revealed will of God. No matter how much the Person and work of the Holy Spirit may be emphasized by such an individual, the Holy Spirit is dishonored and grieved if His instructions are brushed aside.

The second general rule has to do with order in the meetings of God's people. Confusion and disorderliness are alien to the Spirit of God (see I Cor. 14:26,33). A good deal of confusion and disharmony marked the meetings in Corinth as a result of speaking in tongues.

Specific Rules

The first of these is found in I Corinthians 14:6: "Now, brethren, if I come unto you speaking with tongues, what shall I profit you, except I shall speak to you either by revelation, or by knowledge, or by prophesying, or by doctrine?" This means that Bible truth must be given if the tongues gift is employed in the way God intends it to be employed. The Word of God benefits the hearers. Through the Word the Spirit of God works in the hearts of His people.

A good question to ask ourselves with regard to any claim of speaking in tongues is this: "Is the Word of God expounded as a result of this gift? Are people being built up in the faith which was delivered to the saints? Is Christ being exalted?" If the answer to these questions is no, then we must question if the Spirit of God is causing the tongues speaking.

Second, the tongues gift should be used for the edification of the whole church and not be limited to the personal benefit of the person with the gift (see vv. 2,12). Spirit-given gifts are not playthings. They are not to be used selfishly but for the building up of the Body of Christ. The believer is not his own; he has been bought with a price. Any spiritual gift he receives is not for his private entertainment or benefit but for the good of all believers with whom he has contact.

Third, in a group where all, including the one speaking in tongues, spoke the same language, someone had to interpret the message. He was either to be his own interpreter, or someone else was to interpret for him. Otherwise, the tongues speaker was to remain silent (v. 28).

This gift would be of great benefit to foreign missionaries, who must spend months and even years in learning a new language. Some of them, in fact, have to learn several new languages in the course of their missionary work.

At the turn of this century some enthusiastic and earnest Christians went to the mission field with the firm conviction that they had the gift of tongues. They believed it would not be necessary for them to learn the language of the people to whom they would minister. These would-be missionaries were sadly disillusioned. Many of them became spiritual wrecks as a result of their disappointment. The fault did not lie with God but with them and the teachers who had misinterpreted the Scriptures with regard to the gift of tongues.

A fourth rule is that private praying in a tongue was not to be encouraged unless the one who prayed understood what he was praying about. The standard Paul laid down was that one should pray not only with the human spirit but also with the understanding (vv. 14,15).

A fifth rule is that a definite order was to be maintained when the gift of tongues was exercised in a public meeting. No more than three tongues speakers were to take part in any one service and then only one at a time with someone to interpret (v. 27). Since only one was to interpret, this in itself would tend to keep several tongues speakers from trying to speak at the same time. Confusion would be eliminated, and one of the disorders accompanying the zeal of those employing the gift would be corrected.

We have already considered the fact that if a believer employed the gift of tongues, he was to give Bible truth. When this admonition was given to the Corinthians, more than one miraculous gift was needed in order to protect believers from false prophets, and this is the sixth rule. Paul said, "If I come unto you speaking with tongues, what shall I profit you, except I shall speak to you either by revelation, or by knowledge, or by prophesying, or by doctrine?" (v. 6).

Bible truth, or new truth from God, was to be given if the hearers were to be edified. In this way the gift of prophecy would be joined with the gift of tongues. This meant that not only would the rules governing tongues be employed, but an additional rule governing prophecy would also have to be followed.

This particular rule is given in verse 29: "Let the prophets speak two or three, and let the other judge." The function of a judge in this case would be the discerning of spirits, because in the days before the New Testament was complete, additional truth would be revealed from time to time. But, along with this, the danger of the introduction of false doctrine also existed. A check on the teaching of the prophets was needed, because evil spirits could interject false teaching. This judge, then, would try the spirits, and he would need the gift of the discerning of spirits for this.

In a situation of this nature three miracle gifts were needed—the gifts of tongues, prophecy and the discerning of spirits. Does this not indicate that if one miracle gift is to be used today, several or even all of them are needed to keep the rest in balance? The gift of tongues is greatly emphasized, but what of the other gifts? Mark 16:17 is often referred to as proof that the gift of tongues is a sign that will follow believers. But why pick out that one gift and ignore the casting out of demons, the handling of serpents, the drinking of deadly poison or the healing of the sick? And do not overlook another gift spoken of in Matthew 10:8—raising the dead!

A seventh rule is given in I Corinthians 14:32: "The spirits of the prophets are subject to the prophets." This principle applied to the tongues speakers also. The expression of their gift was not beyond their control. It was their responsibility to use it wisely and in an orderly way. Too often God is blamed for what is really the believer's own lack of restraint.

Eighth, a very serious consequence to the use of tongues without an interpreter is dealt with in verses 21-25. This is a portion that has not always been clearly understood.

The apostle emphasizes in this chapter that spiritual gifts are to be used for the edification of the believers. Obviously, believers could not be edified if they could not understand the language being used. But what would be the effect on unbelievers who attended the church services? This is the subject Paul dealt with in these verses.

He wrote: "In the law it is written, With men of other tongues and other lips will I speak unto this people; and yet for all that will they not hear me, saith the Lord. Wherefore tongues are for a sign, not to them that believe, but to them that believe not: but prophesying serveth not for them that believe not, but for them which believe. If therefore the whole church be come together into one place, and all speak with tongues, and there come in those that are unlearned, or unbelievers, will they not say that ye are mad? But if all prophesy, and there come in one that believeth not, or one unlearned, he is convinced of all, he is judged of all: and thus are the secrets of his heart made manifest; and so falling down on his face he will worship God, and report that God is in you of a truth" (vv. 21-25).

The first question we want to answer is "In what sense are tongues a sign to unbelievers?"

The answer is found in this portion. The word "law" refers to the Old Testament, and the passage quoted in Isaiah 28:11,12. When the messages of

140

the prophets were resisted by hard-hearted unbelievers among the Israelites, God warned that He would judge them by sending foreign invaders into their land. These men would speak languages unknown to the Israelites, and the presence of these conquerors would be proof of God's retributive judgment on His people who would not believe in spite of this sign. They would "not hear" the Lord. Consequently, the uninterpreted tongue was a judicial sign to unbelievers. The uninterpreted tongue would indicate judgment on the unbelieving and would not be a means of leading them to faith in Christ.

This was the very opposite of what God intended at Corinth. It stands to reason that the unbelievers who visited the meetings of the Christians in Corinth were not hardened against truth but were seeking spiritual help.

The Greek word for "unbelievers" in verse 22 is the same as the word used for "unbelievers" in verse 23. But the context indicates that the unbeliever in verse 22 is different from the unbeliever of verse 23. Tongues were a judicial sign against hardened unbelievers. But in their meetings the Corinthians probably would not have been dealing with hardened unbelievers but with unbelievers who were apparently seeking spiritual help. By using the gift of tongues without an interpreter present, they were misrepresenting God's attitude toward these lost persons. Another bad result of the uninterpreted tongues would be that the unbelievers attending the services would think God's people were mentally unbalanced.

Still others—the "unlearned" (v. 23)—were adversely affected by the uninterpreted tongues. The

141

word "unlearned" in the original primarily meant a private person rather than a public official. In this context it denotes a person or persons who, though saved, were untaught or unlearned as far as tongues were concerned. So, like the unbelievers of verse 23, these unlearned persons would consider the foreign language used by the tongues speakers as mere gibberish and would think the speakers were not emotionally stable.

God's purpose in giving out His Word is to reach the unsaved and bring them to a saving knowledge of Christ. In addition, it helps the believers grow in grace and in the knowledge of their Lord. He does this by reaching the understanding through intelligible words and appealing to the conscience at the same time. God's Word is heard through the speaker, but if the speaker uses language that is not understood by his hearers, then God's purpose cannot be carried out. To declare that a person is judged (v. 24) means that his heart is searched by the Word and he is inwardly sifted. Each successive speaker in the assembly who speaks in the power of the Holy Spirit deepens the work of the Spirit in these individual hearts.

Verse 25 shows the third stage in this person's conversion if he is an unbeliever: The secrets of his heart are made manifest. First, his true condition is revealed. According to verse 24 he stands self-condemned and sees his own thoughts, motives and desires in their true light. He is awakened to his need and falls down before God.

Finally, women were forbidden to speak in the public assemblies. Connected as this thought is with the subject of tongues, it is very apparent that the women were not allowed to speak in tongues in the early church (see vv. 34,35).

One is forced to admit in light of these rules that, although Paul said, "Forbid not to speak with tongues" (v. 39), he was not strongly encouraging the use of the gift. He left room for the Holy Spirit, however, to exercise His sovereign will in the matter. People tend to go to extremes, and when a doctrine of the Word is misused, many believers avoid it or oppose it. But if the Lord were to throw out every doctrine that people have misapplied or abused, we would have no Bible left.

The New Testament indicates that it was the purpose of God to suspend the use of the miraculous gifts, at least in general, but not because they had been used in the wrong way. Until God suspended their use, the believers were to have freedom in exercising them.

Chapter 11

Temporal and Eternal Gifts

In this chapter we shall see from the Scriptures why God at times permitted gifts which served as signs to the early church and why they were given for a limited time only.

In order to fully understand the subject of I Corinthians 14, it is necessary to distinguish between gifts of a temporary nature and gifts of an eternal nature.

It is also important for us to understand that there is a difference between the gifts of the Holy Spirit and the fruit of the Spirit. Gifts are given for the performance of certain services, and many of them can be imitated by Satan. The fruit of the Holy Spirit, those attributes of righteousness which are the result of the presence of the Spirit of God in the Christian, cannot be imitated by Satan. Remember also that love is the basis for the proper administration of the gifts.

The Eternal Gift

In I Corinthians 13:8-13 Paul made a distinction between the temporary gifts and the eternal one, which is love. "Charity [love] never faileth: but whether there be prophecies, they shall fail;

144

whether there be tongues, they shall cease; whether there be knowledge, it shall vanish away. For we know in part, and we prophesy in part. But when that which is perfect is come, then that which is in part shall be done away. When I was a child, I spake as a child, I understood as a child, I thought as a child: but when I became a man, I put away childish things. For now we see through a glass, darkly; but then face to face: now I know in part; but then shall I know even as also I am known. And now abideth faith, hope, charity, these three; but the greatest of these is charity [love]."

Although other qualities will cease, love will never cease. It is the eternal quality of the Holy Spirit. We possess only the "earnest," or "down payment," of love now. In eternity our hearts will be filled with the same love with which God loved us when He gave His only begotten Son.

To me the sweetest thing in heaven will be my having a heart filled with the love of Christ so that I can love those who I think are unlovable now. Even though I think I cannot love some people here on earth, I will be able to love them in heaven with God's love. And everybody will love me. That will be wonderful! Remember that to a certain degree we possess this love now (Rom. 5:5), but the full measure awaits our glorification. Love, then, is an eternal quality which will be fulfilled in us only when we are in heaven.

The Temporary Gifts

In I Corinthians 13:13 Paul mentioned three gifts—faith, hope and love. Love is the only gift that is endless. Faith will be turned into sight, and

145

hope will become reality; therefore, faith and hope will cease. But love will never end.

All other gifts mentioned in Scripture are also limited by a time element. This includes the three specific gifts mentioned in I Corinthians 13:8: "Whether there be prophecies, they shall fail; whether there be tongues, they shall cease; whether there be knowledge, it shall vanish away."

Prophecy

"Prophecies . . . shall fail" (I Cor. 13:8). The word "prophecy" has a much broader meaning than that of "teaching" or "knowledge." It means both the foretelling of future events and the forthtelling of God's message. This includes preaching the Word in such a way that it brings conviction to hearts.

Prophecy was fragmentary in Paul's day. He said, "We prophesy in part" (v. 9). The Lord revealed one truth with present or future significance to one prophet and another truth to another prophet. "A time will come," Paul said, in effect, "when that which is perfect, or mature, will come; then that which is fragmentary shall cease."

Paul's words were partially fulfilled when the Scriptures, as we have them today, were completed. God's revelation was given in fragments to many different individuals. However, when the revelation became complete, that phase of prophecy which had to do with the foretelling of events was no longer needed. One phase of prophecy—forthtelling, or the giving forth of God's message to bring conviction—continues in our day, but it will not be needed, at least in the sense we now know it, after the end of the Church Age.

Knowledge

Paul said that knowledge would also cease. "Knowledge" means "the understanding of revelation." However, he pointed out that even knowledge is now fragmentary. The Old Testament prophets did not always understand their own prophecies. But God gave some people the gift of knowledge so they could understand and interpret these revelations. A time is coming when the whole truth of Scripture will be revealed to us and the need for the gift of knowledge will cease. For believers this will probably happen at the Rapture.

Tongues

The third specific gift mentioned as being temporary is tongues. The meaning of the word "tongues" is "languages." The gift of tongues (languages) was given so that the gospel might be spread very quickly during the first generation of the Christian era. Paul indicated that the time would come when this gift would no longer be necessary.

"When I was a child, I spake as a child, I understood as a child, I thought as a child: but when I became a man, I put away childish things" (I Cor. 13:11).

Paul was trying to show that when a Christian comes to full maturity and his faith grows stronger, he no longer needs signs. Signs are for children or

147

for those of little faith, but a mature Christian has put away childish things.

Paul illustrated this truth in I Corinthians 14:20: "Brethren, be not children in understanding: howbeit in malice be ye children, but in understanding be men." As far as evil is concerned, we should be as innocent as little children, but as far as knowledge is concerned, we should think like adults.

Seeking the Gifts

In I Corinthians 1:7 Paul said, "So that ye come behind in no gift." The Corinthians possessed all the gifts of the Holy Spirit. Nevertheless, he said, in effect, "Among you there is contention and division. Some of you say, 'I am of Paul'; others say, 'I am of Apollos.' Some say, 'I am of Cephas'; others say, 'I am of Christ.' So there is division."

What caused this division? Paul partially answered that question in Chapter 3, verse 1: "And I, brethren, could not speak unto you as unto spiritual, but as unto carnal, even as unto babes in Christ."

In effect, he said, "I should have fed you with meat, but I can feed you only with milk. You are carnal; you have envy, strife and divisions among you." This situation was the result of pride, which had become evident in the church of Corinth. Because of this contention, many were still babes.

Today many believers are remaining babes in Christ, being contentious over something because they do not know what the Scriptures teach. If a doctrine sounds reasonable or if a preacher makes a certain statement, they accept it without studying the Scriptures.

The Corinthians were overemphasizing the miraculous, or sign, gifts, especially the gift of tongues. But Paul urged them to seek the best gifts: "But covet earnestly the best gifts" (12:31). "Follow after charity [love], and desire spiritual gifts, but rather that ye may prophesy" (14:1).

Prophecy, the speaking forth of the Word of God, is that kind of gift. "I would that ye all spake with tongues, but rather that ye prophesied: for greater is he that prophesieth than he that speaketh with tongues" (v. 5). The gift of prophecy, therefore, is the greatest of these gifts.

Chapter 12

The More Excellent Way

The last verse in I Corinthians 12 reads: "But covet earnestly the best gifts: and yet shew I to you a more excellent way" (v. 31). This more excellent way leads right up to Chapter 13. In fact, this verse is really the introduction to it and should not be separated from it by a chapter division.

The apostle is pointing out that the fruit of the Spirit supersedes the gifts of the Spirit. The fruit of the Spirit is described in Galatians 5:22,23 and may be summarized in one word—love. Love leads the list, with joy, peace, longsuffering, gentleness, goodness, faith, meekness and temperance following.

The love spoken of here, however, is not mere human love. Love is a common word among us today and is often used carelessly by the man on the street as well as by the man in the pulpit. But the love of the Spirit is beyond human attainment. It is a divine love according to Romans 5:5. This love is shed abroad in our hearts by the Holy Spirit. It is one of the results of salvation provided for all who have been justified in Christ. And this is the love that I Corinthians 13 describes. Paul shows here that unless these spiritual gifts are administered in the love of the Spirit, they are valueless.

The problem in Corinth was that men were seeking to use gifts without making sure their own inner hearts were spiritually in tune with God. The fruit of the Spirit was not in evidence. So the use of the spiritual gifts became a source of controversy and competition.

Love Essential

It is this point that Paul emphasized in I Corinthians 13:1 when he said, "Though I speak with the tongues of men and of angels, and have not charity, I am become as sounding brass, or a tinkling cymbal." The word "charity" here is the word "love," and as we have indicated, it is the strong word for love. This is not human love but divine love. It is the love that the Holy Spirit has shed abroad in our hearts. Consequently, though we speak in the languages of men or in the languages of angels and have not love, we are nothing but noisy brass utensils. Spiritual gifts are good if they are ministered in love. Without love, they lead to pride and conceit, to self-praise, to jealousy and slandering of others and even to lying.

Some people are contentious about these gifts even today. But the Bible says that unless we have love along with such gifts, we are nothing. The fruit of the Spirit in the life is the proof of the controlling of the life by the Holy Spirit. Some try to change this by saying that the presence of the spiritual gifts is the evidence of the Spirit's filling. But the actual proof lies in the fruit of the Spirit. This is not something that can be produced naturally by any of us. It takes an apple tree to produce an apple, and it takes the Spirit of God to produce the spiritual fruit that is the evidence of His presence in the heart.

151

If the gifts of the Spirit are not administered in love, the gifts themselves are probably imitations. Satan can enter in and very cleverly deceive us. He can imitate many of the gifts mentioned in I Corinthians 12,13 and 14, but he can neither imitate nor produce the fruit of the Spirit.

The Book of Exodus contains proof of this. When Moses and Aaron appeared before Pharaoh, they performed some miracles. They did this on the basis of wonderful, spiritual powers God had given them. But the sorcerers of Egypt imitated some of the things that Moses and Aaron were using to prove the presence and power of God. Of course, the Egyptians could do this only up to a certain point. But it is possible for Satan to imitate some of these outstanding and spectacular gifts. Consequently, the test concerning the presence of the Spirit in the life lies in another realm. Love, part of the fruit of the Spirit, is the true test.

Do not misunderstand what we are saying here. This is no statement of opposition to the gifts of the Spirit. But we need to remember that Satan can imitate some of these things. He has done it in the past, and there is no doubt that he is doing it again today.

Paul was not content to use the gift of tongues as an illustration, but he also spoke of prophecy, the understanding of mysteries and all knowledge and faith. He showed that without love, all these are useless.

We have noted before that this love of the Spirit is a result of a person's being born again through the Spirit into God's family. The secret of the exhibition of this love lies in the fact that we are indwelt by Christ and He lives this life in us.

Galatians 2:20 says, "I am crucified with Christ: nevertheless I live; yet not I, but Christ liveth in me: and the life which I now live in the flesh I live by the faith of the Son of God, who loved me, and gave himself for me."

Love Implanted

This is not a love that we wait for after we are saved. It is something that is put into our hearts the moment we believe. When the Holy Spirit comes to dwell within, He implants in us the love of God (Rom. 5:5). Love is already in our lives doing this divine work.

In Romans 8:9, we learn that if we are not the recipients of His Spirit, we do not belong to God at all. But when we are His, the Spirit has come and placed the love of God in our hearts. This, then, makes it possible for the fruit of the Spirit—love, joy, peace and these other things listed in Galatians 5:22,23—to be seen in us.

Even though the love of God has been poured into our hearts by the Holy Spirit, it cannot be seen or witnessed by others until we surrender our hearts to the Lord. God has given us a divine nature, a new nature, and through the Holy Spirit, the old nature is overcome. The new life in Christ is seen in us. When we surrender to the Holy Spirit, He takes control. And when He has control, He is able to let the love of God flow through us.

Paul, in his letter to the Ephesians, wrote: "That he [God] would grant you, according to the riches of his glory, to be strengthened with might by his Spirit in the inner man; that Christ may dwell in your hearts by faith; that ye, being rooted and grounded in love, may be able to comprehend with all saints what is the breadth, and length, and depth, and height; and to know the love of Christ, which passeth knowledge, that ye might be filled with all the fulness of God" (3:16-19).

We should not be swept off our feet by the talk of love that people indulge in today. The average person knows nothing of the love of God. Such a person thinks merely of human love. Though that can help in many situations, what we need is supernatural love that goes beyond anything human love can accomplish. For this reason Paul prayed for the inworking of the Holy Spirit and for the filling of the believers' hearts with God's love. By faith, we must recognize that Christ dwells within and that the love of God is shed abroad in our hearts through the ministry of the Holy Spirit.

Rooted and Grounded in Love

In the third place, we are to be rooted and grounded in love, which comes only through daily reading of, and meditating on, the Word and praying in the Spirit. Only as this is done can the Word of God permeate our souls and change us into the likeness of Christ. The final plea here is that we might comprehend, or appropriate, these things by faith. The love of God is magnificent. It is far-reaching. Paul speaks of its length, breadth, height and depth—a four-dimensional love, so great that no individual can appropriate it all or know it all in this life. Together with all saints, however, we can attain to certain portions of it.

It is also a love which passes knowledge. It cannot be fully known, but it can be known and enjoyed far beyond anything any of us have yet experienced. God, in His nature, is love. To be filled with the fullness of God is to be filled with that love.

We are also told in the Scriptures that we are to love God with all our hearts, all our souls and all our minds (Matt. 22:37). Humanly speaking, this is impossible. But, with the work of the Holy Spirit within us, it is an attainable goal. Furthermore, this love is not only to be manifested toward God but also toward those around us. And this will be the proof of the love in our hearts. Our love toward Him will be seen in our love for other people. The vertical relationship of our love to God is proved by the horizontal relationship of love to man. We cannot say we love God unless we love our fellow-man.

John makes this very clear in his Epistle. He says, "No man hath seen God at any time. If we love one another, God dwelleth in us, and his love is perfected in us" (I John 4:12). He also says, "If a man say, I love God, and hateth his brother, he is a liar: for he that loveth not his brother whom he hath seen, how can he love God whom he hath not seen? And this commandment have we from him, That he who loveth God love his brother also" (vv. 20,21). In other words, if we say we love God and yet do not love our brother in the Lord, we are lying. This is the acid test of true spirituality.

This is where Christian leaders and Christian people often clash. There may be disagreements over issues or over principles, but when there is true love, we will not allow them to affect our relationship with others.

Chapter 13

Love Described

Let us reexamine I Corinthians 13 and look more closely at love. Love is like a prism which breaks light into its component parts. Just as the sun shining on mist produces a rainbow, so the light of God shining on His love shows us its various elements.

This chapter should serve as a mirror for us so that we can see for ourselves if we measure up to this love. Most of us, before we go to work in the morning, check our appearance to see if everything is in order. A spiritual checkup is also called for; we need to examine ourselves.

Verses 4 through 7 list 16 components of love. These, we must remember, can never be imitated or produced by the natural man. They are seen only in the lives of believers who have given their hearts over to the Spirit's control.

This section of Scripture reads: "Charity suffereth long, and is kind; charity envieth not; charity vaunteth not itself, is not puffed up, doth not behave itself unseemly, seeketh not her own, is not easily provoked, thinketh no evil; rejoiceth not in iniquity, but rejoiceth in the truth; beareth all things, believeth all things, hopeth all things, endureth all things. Charity never faileth."

156

Patient

We learn first that love is patient. Four different statements are made concerning this. Love, we are told, suffers long, or is "long tempered." It forbears for long periods, and this means there is no room for impatience. Love willingly endures evil and is not hurried but is calm. It is always ready to work when the summons to work is given.

We learn also that it bears all things. There is no limit to its endurance. It overlooks faults in others and does not complain. It does not expose its grief and tears but obscures them from others. It knows how to be silent, how to avoid resentment, how to endure hurt and sorrow without divulging to the world its distresses. Selfishness might prompt a believer to give in to his feelings under hardships, but love enables him to endure patiently.

Hopeful

We also learn that love hopes all things. It hopes under all kinds of circumstances. It is optimistic and not gloomy. It does not look on the dark side of life, nor does it give in to despair or despondency. Anxiety does not affect it. Where true love is, personal woes must go.

It endures all things. A mother's love for her child illustrates this well. Many mothers will go to great lengths to nourish and protect their children, but the love of God is even greater than human love. It has power to do anything. It stands its ground when there seems to be no cause for hope. It endures even when the believers are persecuted for the good they have done. How do we measure up to such love?

Kind

Then we learn that love is kind. It looks for ways to be constructive. It leaves no room for unkindness. It is always gentle. It confers blessing and not condemnation. It seeks to do good to others and not harm. It actively seeks the happiness of others. Our best example, of course, is Christ Himself.

It makes no distinction among persons but is kind toward all. In the midst of sorrow it causes one to have joy. This is possible only because we have the mind and the nature of Christ. We are too inclined to live under the domination of our fallen natures which, of course, have no semblance of such love.

Generous

We find also that love is generous. It never boils over with jealousy. It is not possessive like a child who claims that everything belongs to him. It seeks the advantage of others rather than personal advantage. It causes each of us to treat others better than ourselves. We learn not to count anything as our own but to realize that all we have really belongs to Christ. We do not envy others for the work they are doing for the Lord but rejoice at their success.

Love also is helpful. It does not boast about itself. It is not puffed up. Thus, humility seals our lips so that we forget to tell others of the good we have done. Love hides even from itself. It teaches

158

us to do deeds of kindness, then not to parade them and even to forget we have done them.

This love never boasts or brags. It does not show off its gifts. It is not out for display. It does not try to impress others and is not boastful and self-assertive. It does not seek a special place for itself or push itself forward. The outward expression of love is done in humility.

Inwardly, it is not puffed up. It does not show arrogance. It is not conceited and does not cherish inflated ideas of its own importance. It is teachable and willing to learn. There is an absence of greed and an absence of party zeal and pride, which so characterize the natural man.

Courteous

Love is courteous. It does not behave rudely. This is true in relation to society, small things or great things. The most untutored person moving in the highest society with such love in his heart will behave himself without show. It makes a true lady or gentleman of a believer. It makes one do things gently, not inconsiderately or unsympathetically. It produces good and noble manners. Such love is never rude.

Unselfish

Love is not selfish. It does not seek its own good or insist on its own rights. Paul wrote: "Let this mind be in you, which was also in Christ Jesus" (Phil. 2:5). We are to reckon ourselves dead to the self-nature. For this very reason, we will not insist on our own way. Self-seeking and selfishness are the basis of all evil actions, but love does not seek even that which is its own. It not only gives up its rights but also fails to even seek those rights. The Bible asks, "Seekest thou great things for thyself?" And the admonition is, "Seek them not" (Jer. 45:5).

Greatness lies in unselfish love, not in things. It is more difficult to give up rights we have sought. So it is better that we do not seek them to begin with. Happiness lies not in having or getting but in giving. The Lord said, "Whosoever will be great among you, let him be your minister; and whosoever will be chief among you, let him be your servant" (Matt. 20:26,27). That is true love.

Long Tempered

Love has a good temper. That is, love is not easily provoked to anger. It is not touchy or irritable. It refuses to take offense and does not dwell on having suffered wrong. Anger and wrath are not elements of love and neither is bitterness. The person who is controlled by the love of Christ is not a bitter person. Just as a spark which falls into the ocean is extinguished by the water, so all bitterness is extinguished in this ocean of love. Any evil falling on the heart full of love will be put out without harming the life.

We are inclined to speak of a bad temper as a mere weakness, an infirmity of our nature. A person who is easily angered, one who is quick tempered, harms himself in many other ways. A quick temper leaves one unguarded and reveals that love in the character is missing. Such a disposition ruins homes, society, church life and even national life.

160

Prominent men who have uncontrolled tempers are in some respects mere babies.

An uncontrolled temper is probably harder to live with than any other characteristic. Temper is a symptom of the unloving nature. One unguarded, hasty word does more harm than many other acts of sin. Only as the heart is filled with the love of Christ can a quick temper be overcome.

Thinks No Evil

Love thinks no evil. It is a rare thing, indeed, when a person attributes no evil motives to another but assumes the best motives for the other person's actions. True love does not harbor evil thoughts. It is not suspicious of what the other person is trying to do. Neither does it remember injuries. It does not take into account the wrong suffered. It does not brood over wrong. It bears no malice and is not resentful. That is love.

Love believes all things. It does not do things that will destroy trustful fellowship among believers or individuals. It has confidence in others and does not stand in critical and unkind judgment, attributing to others faults that may not be there or may be exaggerated. It appreciates the good it finds in others and takes the kindest possible view toward what they are doing. It is the very opposite of slander and gossip and the smearing of character so prevalent at times, even among Christians.

Sincere

Finally, love is sincere. It does not rejoice in iniquity but rejoices in the truth. This is not only a matter of rejoicing in what is true with regard to Bible doctrine, but it means that a person seeks to get to the bottom of the facts regarding any situation that may arise. It seeks out truth with humbleness of heart and with unbiased mind. It does not seek to capitalize on another person's faults, nor does it delight in exposing another person's weaknesses. Love covers a multitude of sins (see I Pet. 4:8). Love is glad when good is done but not when evil is done.

Love does not suspect evil in a person under affliction. Job provides an illustration. His so-called friends accused him of harboring wrong and said this was why he suffered. This, we know from the Scriptures, was not the truth. True love never rejoices when judgment falls on a person for evildoing but is glad when God shows mercy. Neither does it excuse sin in one's own life. True love enables us to see goodness and evil as the Lord sees them.

Never Fails

Last of all, love never fails. When all else fails, love is still there. The great fact for the Christian to grasp is that the love of God has been shed abroad in his heart by the Holy Spirit.

The opening words of Chapter 14 state that the Christian is to follow after love and to desire spiritual gifts, especially the gift of prophecy. These two admonitions make a fitting conclusion to Chapters 12 and 13. We are to exercise love in everything. The gifts of the Spirit without the grace of the Spirit are ineffective in providing spiritual help to others. Prophecy is the outstanding gift for ministering to others. It edifies, exhorts and comforts, but only as it is administered in love.

We must ask ourselves, "Is this love being practiced in my life? If not, why not?" If our hearts are not filled with love, it is because we are not filled, or controlled, by the Holy Spirit. What we need to do, then, is to surrender ourselves entirely to the Spirit of God so that He can show in and through us this love of Christ. May God search our hearts and cause us to come to Him in full obedience to His will and yield ourselves completely to His control!